One Mort

One Mortal Night

A Miscarriage of Justice

Patrick Kelleher

SOMERVILLE PRESS

Somerville Press
Dromore, Bantry,
Co. Cork, Ireland

Designed by Jane Stark
Typeset in Adobe Garamond
seamistgraphics@gmail.com

ISBN: 978 0 9562231 1 1

Printed in Spain

'This was a goodly person,
Till the disaster that, one mortal night,
Drove him to this.'

SHAKESPEARE, *PERICLES*, ACT V, SCENE 1, 36

The author and publisher would like to thank the following organizations for permission to quote from work still in copyright: Boosey and Hawkes Music Publishers Ltd for permission to quote from the song 'I hear you calling me', p.59; R. Dardis Clarke, executor of the Austin Clarke Literary Estate, 17 Oscar Square, Dublin 8 for permission to quote from the poem 'The Planter's Daughter', p.76; John Murray (Publishers) for permission to quote from the poem 'A Subaltern's Love Song', from *Collected Poems* by John Betjeman © 1955, 1958, 1964, 1968, 1970, 1979, 1981, 1982, 2001, p.79; The Trustees of the Estate of the late Katherine B. Kavanagh, through the Jonathan Williams Literary Agency, to quote the stanzas from 'On Raglan Road' by Patrick Kavanagh, which are reprinted from *Collected Poems*, edited by Antoinette Quinn (Allen Lane 2004), p.215.

ACKNOWLEDGEMENTS

I acknowledge the assistance of the late Michael O'Dwyer, Tom O'Donnell, Terry Fennessy, Gerard O'Connell, Ken Bergin, Donal Murphy, Mike Hackett, Stephen McNeill, John Duncan, Dr Marie Murray, Frances Wrafter, Miriam Kirby, David, James and Cathy Kelleher, Ann Grassick and the Pallasgreen and Offaly Historical Societies.

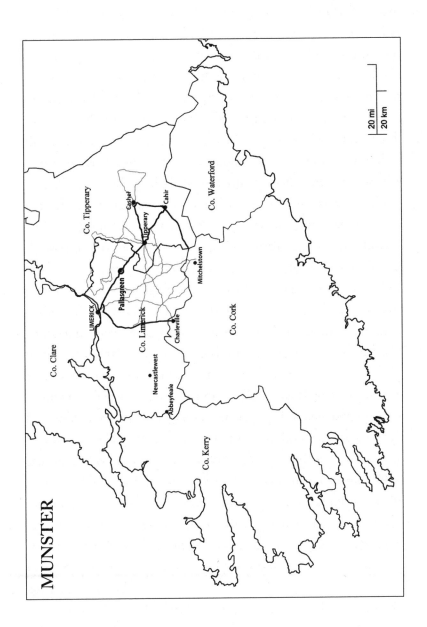

MUNSTER

Co. Clare

Co. Tipperary

Co. Waterford

LIMERICK

Cashel

Tipperary

Cahir

Pallasgreen

Co. Limerick

Mitchelstown

Newcastlewest

Charleville

Abbeyfeale

Co. Cork

Co. Kerry

20 mi
20 km

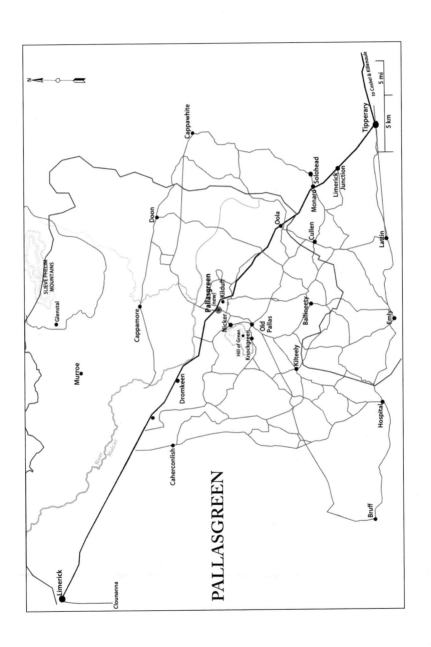

PALLASGREEN

CHAPTER 1

He was strong and wiry and moved with the speed and suddenness of a panther as Jamie, my younger brother, and I entered. Then, like a coiled spring, his hands guarding his face, he danced menacingly around the day room of the old police barracks. He jabbed his left fist with a rapid repeated action into the panelled walls of the building, the rat-tat-tat sound echoing around its vast emptiness. Head down, he feinted first one way, then another, his hair falling over his handsome brow. Sometimes, unexpectedly, he threw a right hand, then a left, then a right again as if pummelling an opponent into submission. Finally, he delivered a vicious right uppercut to his imaginary rival and danced away quickly, his expression triumphant, as he watched his victim, as it were, sink to his knees, only to fall prostrate on the bare boards of the barrack day room.

Then, grinning, he turned to us, his fans, as we roared our approval. But the performance was not over yet. He sat down quickly by the window and threw back his head, exposing his powerful neck. It seemed to us to ripple with muscles. He pointed to it. 'Look at that, lads,' he said excitedly. 'Feel it, feel it; it's like a steel rope, isn't it?'

We touched its muscular whiteness ever so lightly and then, incredulous, we answered in unison.

'Gosh, it is. How did you do it?'

'Training,' he answered quickly, then went on. 'And do you know something else, lads? They couldn't hang me even if they tried.'

We recoiled for a moment at the thought of the young garda ever finding himself in such a predicament. But then we put it out of our minds quickly as he laughed out loud at our bemused faces and resumed punching the air again and ramming his fists into the shuddering woodwork.

He sat down beside the phone that rarely ever rang and pulled out some plain white sheets of paper. It seemed he spent hours sketching famous people in the news to fill the tedium on the days when he took his turn as barrack orderly in a village where nothing much happened. Given his extraordinary energy, maybe one day he would make it happen.

Over the fireplace one such sketch had pride of place. She was a very beautiful woman. He admitted that she fascinated him, not only because of her beauty and enigmatic expression but also, he said, in light of her extraordinary motherly quality. 'And yet,' he said wistfully, 'she loves a man scarcely deserving of her.' He tantalizingly withheld her name. He gazed at her for a long time in silence and then, before turning abruptly back to the table, his lips quietly formed her name: Eva Braun. He could not bring himself to utter the name of her lover, Adolf Hitler.

He began sketching, with sure strokes, some of the great heavyweight-boxing champions of the era, whom he knew Jamie and I admired. He gave them appropriate captions: The Brown Bomber, The Ambling Alp and The Wild Bull of the Pampas. The likenesses he achieved at great speed were astounding.

As he proceeded, I had an opportunity to study him more closely. His hands were lily-white, slender yet strong. In repose he had the face more of a poet than a policeman, with a broad forehead and large, blue-green, luminous eyes. His fine mop of chestnut hair enhanced his good looks, despite a certain pallor and tenseness about his face. He may still have seemed to be rather boyish, but to us he was, already, almost a god.

He had a gold *fáinne* pinned to his uniform jacket, which glinted now in the late autumn sunshine as it streamed through the large, ever-naked barrack window. Jamie, noting the tiny circle of pure gold, asked him for a poem in Irish for a newspaper competition. He did not hesitate. This time he took out some lined foolscap marked at the top with the legend Saorstát Éireann, and the imprint underneath of the national harp emblem. He began writing furiously. The words flowed from his pen as if he was but a conduit for some ultimate creative force. The handwriting itself, even the arrangement of the lines, all had the mark of perfection. Eventually, after completing six or seven pages, he put the finishing touches to it. Smiling again, he handed the sheets to Jamie, who clutched them to his breast. A poem is a poem is a poem; the author saw no need for explanation. Like a piece of sculpture, it stands alone.

As Jamie and I took our leave of him, he watched from the barrack steps, looking a little forlorn. He clearly enjoyed the company of young people and told us that he came from a large family himself. We waved as we crossed the lawn to our quarters on one side of the building. When we were out of earshot, young Jamie looked up enquiringly.

'Does he really mean that he has trained his neck in case he is ever hanged?' he asked.

'Not really. It's probably just a trick he has perfected.'

Jamie looked relieved. Privately I was not so sure. I had heard it said of multi-talented people that many had uncanny insight not only into their deeper nature but possibly even into the very destiny that awaited them. Could it be, I wondered, that the new recruit, by name Dan Duff, harboured a secret fear that one day that most ultimate of humiliations would befall him?

It was a troubling thought.

CHAPTER 2

When next I met Dan, I was billeted in the disused top room of the barracks, my father, Sergeant Kelleher, having banished me from the family quarters in anticipation of the arrival of a seventh child. It was his strongest hint yet that, since I was now past seventeen, it was near time I was moving on. The room had an iron bed with a hard mattress and several coarse black state-issue blankets that smelt of intense fumigation. Beside it was a lavatory to which late-returning officers tramped up the bare stairway at all hours and tugged violently at the flushing mechanism until the wretched thing finally managed a reluctant ejaculation. The worst nights were at weekends when brawling families exploded into the station around midnight, loudly blaming one another and seeking out 'the sergeant' for his now famous, if unorthodox, powers of mediation between warring factions. On some Saturday nights I did not sleep until dawn.

One summer morning, I went out onto the flat roof to which a narrow doorway led. I breathed the fresh air deeply, trying to recover some equilibrium of mind and body after the deprivations of the night. Suddenly I heard a light step on the landing and there, framed in the doorway, was a young man in a police uniform, open at the neck, his head uncovered and hair somewhat askew. It was Dan, the new recruit. 'Hello, Pat,' he said. 'Good to see you again.'

It appeared that he had just risen. Given his casual, unkempt look that morning, I was struck by the resemblance he bore to a famous film actor, Montgomery Clift, a man whose story I had heard described as the saddest ever told. I knew this actor to be a loner, a misfit and a neurotic perfectionist. I looked for a moment at my newfound friend to see if I could detect in him any such traits. I saw none, but the men were alike in more ways than one. Both had an aura, a mysterious, unfathomable quality. It was this that fascinated, attracted, even perplexed me, with always the possibility of a hidden flaw allied to an infinity of talent.

We surveyed the lush terrain from our vantage-point four storeys up. To the east, at a place called Kilduff, a fine old house surrounded by trees caught the eye. It was known that an old land dispute had erupted there once again; the residents were seeking police protection, but the police authorities at headquarters had sent a young man who had been a mere three months in the service. It was in fact Dan—a boy, the villagers said, on a man's errand. When they came face to face with him in the village, they gasped in disbelief.

As I studied him standing beside me on the barrack rooftop, I could understand the villagers' dismay. He was indeed an unlikely-looking police officer, as I had noted the first day I met him. He seemed eager, however, even enthusiastic, to take on any assignment offered. He was perhaps at that preferred age to send young men to war, because they are then without fear.

He was also, to my eye, a polite, perhaps all too cultivated lad from one of the better schools in County Kildare who had been sent to cut his teeth in a more robust culture than the one to which he had been accustomed. He had probably enlisted because there was little else on offer with the war still on and he with talent to burn. I could have thought of half a dozen other careers he might have pursued with more profit, if only the times were normal. We were later to discover that Dan had a marvellous tenor voice and that alone could have earned him a good living. I got the impression that he believed he had come to some quiet problem-free backwater where nothing much ever arose to ruffle the calm surface of things. He probably had little or no understanding of the depth of feeling aroused by land disputes, especially in the Golden Vale of south Tipperary, east Limerick and north Cork, where the soil was reputedly the richest in all the land.

It looked fine on the surface around Pallasgreen, with gently rolling hills all about, the river meandering charmingly along by the railway, and hardly a soul moving about in the village. But if you were a newcomer, especially a rookie policeman, and you put a foot wrong, you quickly got your comeuppance.

Throughout the land wars some fifty years before, in the 1880s, Pallas was famous for one thing especially: the tenant farmers, more effectively than anywhere else in County Limerick, had taken on the landlords, and had won. The times then were so bad that those young men and women were described by a visiting journalist as the most sullen people he had encountered in all his travels. Well, they had good reason to be sullen, for the landlords in the area held the largest estates in the country, and when evictions took place, it was the police in their hundreds, backed up by armed cavalry, who supported not the hapless tenants, but the landlords. Yet when political independence came and the new force were attired in entirely different uniforms, distrust of the police still ran deep in the psyche of the local people.

But it was not only the land wars that had left their mark on the rugged, if dwindling, population of Pallas. It was always, to its cost, a strategically located village, militarily speaking, being almost exactly halfway between Cashel and Limerick, seats of warring dynasties a thousand years before, which clashed finally at a place called Solohead, just a few miles east of the village. The landscape in between, known as the Mulcair Valley, would be contentious terrain for centuries afterwards.

As we stood together on the barrack rooftop, silently admiring the distant hills and the tranquillity of the village below, I decided I must tell Dan Duff something of that turbulent history and its effect on the people around here, if only to disabuse him of any notion that Pallas was a haven. I had the impression that he saw the picturesque countryside a little too romantically, as a home away from home where he would have time to indulge his artistic side.

I told him that our history teacher often reminded us that fertile though the soil in the area was, under it lay the scars of a bloody history, with ownership still in the hands of the same families who had struggled for centuries to hold on to what was most dear to them—the land. I told him further that, ever since those times, they had tended to distrust the newcomer, the visitor, especially, as our teacher put it, 'if he wore a uniform'.

I pointed out to Dan some of the landmarks of those grim times past. Half a mile west was a reddish ruin that had once been Linfield House, where some of the deadliest confrontations between police and local people took place during the land wars in the 1880s, and beyond it I indicated to him Dromkeen, scene of a horrific ambush in the later Troubles where nine men died, some Tans, some police, all from Pallas Barracks. Even the hills, I told him, had a bitter story to tell. Facing us, a few miles north, were the Slieve Phelims, across which Sarsfield had ridden to a history-making intervention at Ballineety in 1690 and, right behind our backs, a mere half-mile southwards, rose the majestic Hill of Grean (the name derived, ironically, from Grian, an ancient Irish goddess of love) with a Mass Rock on top where fugitive priests had officiated, under deadly threat, in penal times.

To my surprise and dismay, Dan seemed not all that moved by my stories, flinching briefly only when I recounted some of the grim details of what had happened at Dromkeen in February 1921. It was a cunningly laid trap by the local Volunteers: a quiet spot where three roads met; a sharp bend forcing the convoy to slow down; riflemen took aim from all angles. It was a near massacre. Against the odds, I told him, two men had scrambled free and made it back to the barracks, firing their guns in the air as they came in to alert their colleagues to be ready to hasten to that lonely crossroads where nine of their comrades lay dying.

I recall how Dan turned away abruptly. Perhaps, I reflected, he was one of those people who preferred to live in the here and now, who became impatient with an endless recounting of events that had happened long ago. He seemed more interested in the aesthetic than the historic, as he turned sharply to focus on the once dubbed 'unlovely edifice' on which we were standing. He remarked, with not a little passion, 'All of what you tell me explains, presumably, why this monstrous eyesore was constructed here more as a fortress than as a police station.'

'It does,' I replied, as he lightly touched with his hand one of the giant chimney-stacks.

'There's a strange theory locally', I continued, 'as to how it came to be built so absurdly out of scale with the tiny village: it's said, believe it or not, that the British built it in error to a set of plans meant for Cyprus or even, some say, India.'

'I could well believe it,' he answered dryly. 'It's not too difficult to imagine a careless civil servant, in London probably, with a mere stroke of a pen imposing this hideous thing on a once pretty village.'

I told him that there was an even greater irony in the chequered history of the old barracks in Pallas: 'It was actually burnt down in the Civil War and, lo and behold, the new Free State government, learning nothing from their bungling predecessors, rebuilt it, if anything, larger and uglier than before.'

He threw his eyes to heaven in disbelief as the phone rang deep in the bowels of the building. He made to go. As he did, I found myself doubting that Dan understood the subtext of my history lesson: that he should be wary until he understood better how things worked around Pallas. I had the feeling, however, that caution was not in his nature. He reminded me of certain kinds of men about whom I had read, often poets or artists, whose lust for life was so strong that they could not live without challenge, risk, even danger. I knew that if he was such a man, there was little I could do or say to influence him. The first day I met him, he seemed to blurt out that he believed his fate was determined. 'What will be, will be' appeared to be his philosophy.

Still smiling, Dan slipped back through the narrow doorway. As I heard his light footsteps going quickly down the naked stairway, I looked again at the vast panorama. There was much else that I had not told him: how the Black and Tans had carried out reprisals after Dromkeen, shooting their guns recklessly and flying a home-made flag from the barrack rooftop to taunt the villagers below; how a widowed lady who had lost her husband in the ensuing violence was said to have put a curse on the barracks and all in it, and how the locals had believed subsequently, in the enduring potency of the lady's powers, for the barracks apparently had been dogged by ill luck for years afterwards.

It was this bloody history of the area that caused the villagers to fear the resumption of the old land dispute. They knew it always brought trouble, even tragedy, because passions became so aroused. In the barracks they saw it merely as another job to be done, albeit a tough one; elsewhere there was only foreboding.

Those were my first encounters with Dan Duff. He was one of two heroes of my teenage years, the other being a classmate at secondary school. Both were subjected to tyrannies of a sort, while many of us, myself included, stood idly by. The thought of having failed them both, in their hours of need, has tormented me ever since.

My classmate was a boy cruelly nicknamed 'Spider'. I never knew his true name for no one addressing him ever accorded him that courtesy. But, unlike the hugely talented Duff, Spider was wise. He left school relatively unscathed, having been picked on by a teacher named Murph because he was so tiny and seemingly friendless. He was called Spider because of his thin, pale face, jet-black hair plastered down, black suit and long slender hands. Whatever demons possessed the ogre-faced Murph, who was himself tiny and had never been known to smile, he picked on Spider as if he desperately needed someone smaller than himself on whom to vent his anger and his unhappiness with his lot.

Spider feared telling anyone at home of this horrific treatment at the hands of Murph, who put him in front of the class each day and fired questions about Latin grammar at him so fast that Spider had no time to answer. Murph, warming to this preferred mode of imparting knowledge, clattered Spider first on the left cheek and then on the right, then left again as if he was a punch bag. Spider's tiny head was knocked to and fro, and whenever he tried to duck the blows that rained down on him, Murph hit him even harder for daring to evade his punishment.

But, worst of all, those of us at the back of the class, mostly strongly built sons of guards and farmers and all taller than the diminutive Murph, looked on in silence, never lifting as much as an eyebrow in defence of our beleaguered classmate. True, many of us froze inside and in case we would be barred from school for intervening. But then after some weeks of these horrible beatings, something strange was observable about Spider that seemed to anger Murph all the more. Throughout his torment, his pale face never changed colour despite the battering he was taking; his sleek hair remained unruffled and he never dropped a single tear.

Moreover, he began to maintain defiant eye contact with Murph as he was repeatedly struck, as if to say, 'You bastard. I am not going to let you get the better of me, no matter how you try.' And cowards that we were at the rear of the class, who had helped to undermine Spider earlier by cruelly nicknaming him, now began to admire him as it dawned on us that he was indeed a brave and indomitable boy.

Then on the playground at lunchtime we began to see further amazing changes in Spider's appearance and demeanour. We had not properly noticed before what perfect features he had, with his flawless pallor and finely chiselled face. An artist surely would have viewed him as quite a beautiful boy and so we began to realize that it was perhaps these exceptional qualities that, consciously or unconsciously, Murph disliked and resented in Spider, he himself being so grim-faced.

Soon Spider, now aged about fifteen, came to project a more confident disposition, adopting a pose almost in the way he held his cigarette, and a half-smile played constantly around his lips, as, always alone, he gazed now more contentedly towards the distant hills. Passive resistance was paying off. His new self-possession seemed to madden Murph so much that his face became contorted with rage, for no matter how hard he tried, he could not break Spider. Spider knew he was winning.

His hairstyle, given his new-found confidence, became sleeker, his smile sardonic, his voice deeper, and even in the manner he carried himself he was no longer hesitant and furtive—he was indeed almost cocky. And so the penny dropped with us as to who the model was for his entirely new persona, and we no longer called him Spider but 'Bogie', and we saw him henceforth in a new light and envied his self-possession. Then one day Bogie failed to appear at school, and the next day and the day after that. I never saw him again. Should he chance to read this one day, I would like to say to him, 'Here's looking at you, kid.'

But Dan Duff never showed the slightest intention of quitting the Garda Síochána, though early on the omens were not good for him. I saw him go out on his first solo patrol. Many viewed him as a rising star in the force, but gradually the adulation he received for his magnificent singing and general artistry began to change him. He became the toast of the village and was often penniless from matching his elders drink for drink in the pubs. Soon, he had more the look of the doomed artist than the police officer, burdened as he was by an excess of creative energy and imagination. Dubbed a young genius by many in the village, it was famously said of such a man that, 'he does what he must,' and one felt that Dan would not shrink from doing whatever he thought was necessary in any given situation, no matter how challenging it was.

CHAPTER 3

I watched Dan one afternoon striding briskly out of the station. The eagerness of his step suggested that he was bent on proving himself at the earliest opportunity. I felt not a little sorry for him, because his heavy uniform was buttoned to the neck despite a hot sun. His cap was ill-fitting, making him look a callow and weedy youth; I knew that was not the reality beneath and might tempt foolish men to underestimate him.

He stood for a time at the crossroads, getting his bearings. As I watched, I found it hard to believe that such a talented young man could enjoy earning his living in a uniform, implying, as it did, a rigidity and limitation of mind under which I knew he did not labour. I wondered if deep down he would like to have broken free of it all. But probably he could not, even if he had wanted to, for the forces of social control, which had most of us in the village in one form of straitjacket or another, were simply too powerful.

He looked down the main street. Not a single other human being was in sight. I knew that he would almost certainly avoid the main road going east to Tipperary town and west to Limerick city. The two bye roads leading out of Pallas were more interesting, one going north past the railway and the Mulcair river towards the Slieve Phelim hills, the other going south towards the Hill of Grean with, nestling under it, the two small villages of Old Pallas and Nicker. They were both quiet, narrow roads with dense hedgerows and only the odd farmhouse along the way. They were idyllic to stroll along at that time of year with the warm hum of summer everywhere.

I was not surprised when I saw Dan take the road towards Nicker and Old Pallas, with their shops, pubs and girls as pretty as anywhere else in the area—the O' Tooles, McCormacks, Hartys and Mulcahys. As he walked briskly away from Pallas, I wished I could have joined him and so pointed out to him some of the landmarks that I knew so well. But while I was allowed to mingle freely in the barracks, I was not allowed to go on patrol with an officer. Especially I would have loved to climb the hill and sit with Dan beside the Mass Rock to view the vast lush valley below—there was no place quite like that summit on a sunny afternoon—but I realized we would have to wait for another day to make that pilgrimage together.

What happened Dan soon after was, to say the least, unfortunate. To be so unlucky on his very first patrol must have compounded those fears he seemed to harbour that fate was not on his side. It was later, on returning, that he told me how, unexpectedly, he had become involved in an incident that would have repercussions for him long after.

But first, he said, he had come upon two young ladies, resplendent in their summer dresses, standing chatting beside their bicycles at the side of the road by Nicker school. It was a place I knew well, every inch of it. I can still see the scene, not an unfamiliar one when a new recruit came to the barracks and certain young ladies, on hearing of his arrival, rode out together in the hope of a chance encounter. This pair chose a strategic crossroads to stop and talk a while. It was not long before Dan happened in their direction. They smiled as he approached and soon, as was the prerogative of a young police officer on duty, he engaged them in a mildly flirtatious interrogation which they would, no doubt, have enjoyed.

But that afternoon they were soon interrupted by ominous sounds in the distance, of men shouting and singing lustily and of horses' hooves galloping. One of the girls, he told me, quickly supplied an explanation: 'It must be the Scanlons, the undertakers; they always have a few drinks after a funeral and then they drive like mad. When they bury someone well off especially, they have quite a party afterwards.'

Dan's first reaction was to conclude that, judging by the extent of their merriment, the Scanlons must have interred someone very wealthy indeed. He confessed to being perturbed, however, to note from the young lady's tone that this family of undertakers-cum-cattle dealers seemed to be rather feared locally and yet, in some perverse way, also admired.

Shortly after, they saw a team of horses drawing a hearse coming downhill at a breakneck speed; in the seating at the front of it, singing, shouting and swearing, were three or four men. The driver, Dan said, appeared to be urging the steaming horses on to greater endeavour. Soon they were racing past the school where small children often spilled out at this time of day. Luckily the youngsters had just gone home.

As the cavalcade approached the bend where Dan and the young women were standing, the horses showed no sign of being restrained and the rickety hearse was careering all over the road. Dan managed to shepherd the young women into the safety of the hedge. The hearse, however, bounced off the kerbside and was thrown across the road, catching one of the girls' bicycles and severely warping one of its wheels. They were ashen-faced with fright while the horses raced on, the men still singing and laughing. Though several brothers worked for the Scanlon undertakers, only one, by name Tom, was present that day and was driving the vehicle, while the most vocal of the group was an employee named Power.

A short distance farther on, the group pulled up. As Dan approached them, some members of the group joked about him loudly, noting his extreme youthfulness: 'He's not too long out of short pants, lads,' one said, to loud guffaws. Further insolent remarks and bellowing laughter followed. The young women could hear all this and one of the men then leeringly invited them to join in the banter.

At this point Dan requested the men to step down onto the roadway. They declined, complaining that their horses were tired and must get home. Dan asked them for their names and addresses and they dissolved into laughter at what they perceived to be an idiotic question: 'Sure everyone around here knows us; we're here every other day.'

Their uncooperative and insolent attitude made Dan all the more determined and, no doubt, under that clumsily fitting cap that appeared to diminish him, there was more steel than they could possibly have imagined. He knew that their failure to provide names and addresses entitled him to arrest them forthwith, but realized that if he, the new recruit, were seen leading several men, a hearse and horses through the village, he would become a laughing stock. He decided that he must at all costs secure their names and addresses and so reached a hand up to the driver to help him down which, in his drunken state, the driver mistook for a forgiving handshake. Soon he landed rather unsteadily on the roadway, complaining bitterly of being pulled down, while his associates followed sheepishly. The driver's protests were brushed aside and the charges of reckless driving read out to him. As he was writing down the names and addresses, Dan told me that it occurred to him that, in a manner of speaking, he had met these men before: 'Bullies are bullies the world over,' he said. 'I've met them at school, in the army and, when they are finally confronted, they turn out to have feet of clay.' He was, however, looking sombre as he recounted the story. To compound his dismay, he found on returning to the young women that any rapport he had established with them had vanished.

A young recruit needs, among other things, a little luck in his first posting. It had not come Dan's way that day. I knew the Scanlons only by repute; they had a mixed reputation, but there was a grudging respect for them in the district because of the work they did. God's work, the locals said. Apparently, it was only when they had drink taken that they became troublesome, and a blind eye seems generally to have been turned to their misdemeanours. I saw from Dan's mood, however, that he knew by their attitude that he had not seen the last of them.

On the first day I met him I had made the judgment that, youthful though he may have looked, Dan was not a man to suffer fools and I wondered as he headed into the station, taking the front steps three at a time, if that was necessarily a good thing in a police officer. I wondered too, as I reflected on everything he had told me, if that handshake, that impulsive helping hand offered to the inebriated undertaker, would not some day come back to haunt him.

CHAPTER 4

Haunt him that encounter with the Scanlon group duly did, so much so that Dan Duff's career, his self-belief and his dignity all hung in the balance for several months. And, knowing him, one would have thought that he would have been the last man to make an enemy.

I met him on the evening of the court proceedings standing on the steps at the station entrance. Those steps were a favourite place for an officer to spend time, when in reflective mood, especially late on a summer evening, soothed by all the sounds and sights emanating from the trees that surrounded the old Protestant church opposite. In later years, when I visited Pallas, I was saddened to find that the church and the trees, under whose shadow I had grown up, had been swept away and replaced by a petrol station. That evening I found Dan in a gloomy mood as he gazed intently at the night sky, as if trying to find answers there to the questions that were bothering him.

I sensed that his low mood had its origin in the morning's events. I had heard that the court had found against the Scanlons for dangerous driving, and therefore I wondered why he was dejected. I knew he was not a man to gloat about a success or a victory, if indeed that is what it was. Eventually, I found enough courage to probe the reason for his apparent ill humour.

'How did it go this morning?' I asked tentatively.

'Our Scanlon friends were bound over to keep the peace, but I don't believe it will stop them from making trouble again.'

'But your evidence was accepted in the court, was it not?'

'It was in the court, but the lads inside are not all that enthusiastic.'

'What did they say?'

'James Byrne thinks that I may have stirred up a hornets' nest.'

'What about the others?'

'They were silent and that's what's disappointing.'

'What did they expect you to do, turn a blind eye?'

'I guess so.'

Byrne was a man who tended to hold grudges and assume authority improperly over younger men. He had not forgiven Dan for borrowing his bicycle without permission, by which simple act Dan had made an enemy. And, while Dan believed he could handle the Scanlons if they showed up again, coping with Byrne was a different matter, for the latter was a close friend of the superintendent and his wife. So close was he that he sat with the lady in her quarters when her husband was absent and exercised the great man's coursing hounds every day. This relationship, no doubt, empowered him, as he saw it, to be as hard on Dan as he wanted.

Byrne was one of three middle-aged bachelors with whom twenty-year-old Dan shared the dining hall and dormitory. They were a motley crew. The older men had come into the force when qualifications were few and vocations fewer. It was sufficient then to be able-bodied, to be able to read and write and see ahead of yourself for a reasonable distance. If you had integrity and good character, these would or would not emerge in time. Either way, you would find it hard to get yourself sacked.

One could not, however, be other than sorry for this bachelor trio. In the quarter of a century since they had enlisted in the early 1920s, they had not advanced that much, either personally or professionally. They had no privacy in their lives and, given that the population of the small village of Pallas was not more than a hundred or so, with no active social goings-on there, or transport system out of it, their dearest longings for companionship and a home of their own one day were but a pipedream. Younger men of drive and initiative moved on to other stations, some on promotion, as soon as they had some experience under their belts, and made good. Pallas was a district headquarters station with surplus accommodation and a sergeant who was far from being a disciplinarian. I always believed that this may have been the reason why more than a fair share of misfits were sent to Pallas, the authorities probably knowing that my father, if he found they lacked initiative, would let them be. Besides, he tended to hog to himself any important work, unless he had men available as bright and energetic as Dan. The superintendent had wider responsibilities looking after a number of sub-stations, in an eight-mile radius or so, and tended to leave Father to look after the local scene. For these reasons, the three middle-aged bachelors, having found a cosy, pensionable, nest, were overcome by inertia and had adopted lifestyles that bordered on the bizarre.

Stan Hollis was friendly with Dan, however, but no better a role model for him than Byrne. A tall, once handsome, former star GAA footballer, he had gone to flesh and was no longer motivated in policing work. Instead, he had become a cynic and a playboy. He specialized in derision and nothing inside or outside the station escaped his heartily delivered ridicule. The son of an Englishman, it may have been that Hollis was brought up to believe that the native Irish were unserious about work and responsibility. If that were so, he had stolen our clothes, and in any scale of human fecklessness, few outranked him. Yet I suspected that he saw himself as someone above the ordinary, a man of style, intellect and wit, whom the police service did not deserve.

I had to smile when I watched Hollis, with easy banter, gather round him a poker school when it was his turn to be barrack orderly, the sessions often lasting into the night and occasionally, if one of their number went broke, transferring to Cunningham's pub across the road, where the hapless victim was plied with alcohol to soothe him, before being sent home. Hollis laughed heartily when explaining to his friends what a cushy job he held down at the station and when suggesting, with mock bemusement, what idiots the others were to take it seriously for half a second.

He knew no shame. In later months, after I had done a stint in summer camp with the Local Defence Force, I naively thought I knew it all, including the so-called facts of life. But one of the cruder of those facts I had yet to learn. One evening Dan and Hollis invited me to a police dance in Limerick city, the first I had attended. The hall was packed, hot and sweaty. Hollis was our driver and we had seen him, slightly drunk, dance all night with a young woman half his age. He was somewhat late returning to the squad car, over the 'Garda' sign of which he had thrown an old sack to conceal its identity. As he got into the driving seat, his startling comment left us speechless: 'Jeez, lads,' he blurted, his words slurred, 'if that shagging redhead doesn't have a child after that, she'll never have one.'

The third bachelor member, a man named McCabe, was a horse of a different colour, and if Dan had little rapport with Byrne and Hollis, he had none at all with McCabe, the mystery man of the station. If anyone in the building was seriously under a cloud, it was he. McCabe was confined to clerical work in the station and no one appeared to know whether this was at the insistence of the authorities or at his own request. He padded around the building in soft shoes and a sports coat, looking furtively into rooms and offices. He was often about to say something but changed his mind and left again. He cycled extraordinary distances at weekends—nobody knew where— and returned looking haggard and worn. It seemed as if McCabe forced himself to undertake these punishing marathons to quell whatever demons were struggling inside him for expression that, if let loose, could destroy him.

It was rumoured that there was a secret file concerning McCabe in the station, no doubt under lock and key. No one admitted to knowing exactly what it contained, but it was generally suspected that it may have had to do with his preference for the company of young boys, whom he asked to go with him to the cinema at Cappamore, four miles away. McCabe had already been moved around the country more often than he cared to remember. One false step and he would depart yet again with his bicycle, quietly, on the afternoon train, and since he was a figure more of shadow than substance, no one, outside of his colleagues in the barracks, would notice or ask any questions.

Completing the picture of Pallas barracks, just as the land row started to boil up, were four others. Two were married gardaí, of indifferent health, one near crippled with arthritis, the other so nervous that he used to watch from behind a tree where he lived, opposite the barracks, before venturing into the building, so fearful was he of encountering the superintendent. The super, however was rarely there and, when he was, tended to be preoccupied with his social status, his unhappy, childless wife and his coursing hounds. This left Father, the sergeant-in-charge—impulsive, unorthodox, confrontational—who never belonged in the police in the first place. He was by far the longest-serving officer in the station.

This then was something of the style of policing and the calibre of police officer in Pallas when the station was about to be confronted with one of the most potentially violent land rows in decades. It was known locally that, some time after Christmas, Timmy Cronin would depart the national army, from where he was based in Limerick. He would come to claim his inheritance and to build a home on the family farm at nearby Kilduff. He had let it be known that he would kick up the mother and father of all rows to secure his just entitlement. Reputedly a crack shot when in the army, his behaviour could be unpredictable. It was a lethal combination and all the more deadly for the fact that he was said to be cultivating paramilitary connections.

Neither Father nor the superintendent were ideally suited to preside over the crisis to come, having been lulled into a false sense of security by the almost total absence of crime during the Emergency years. Father had already been twelve years in Pallas and the superintendent only two and it was difficult to guess which of the pair would be blamed, if the protection duty assignment went badly wrong. Time alone would tell.

Father, however, had had a tough upbringing, for he was a child of the Troubles, having been reared in the garrison town of Youghal, County Cork, where confrontation was in the very air. His ardently nationalistic mother urged him and his five brothers to join the cause and, if necessary to die for it; she claimed kinship with the Fenian Jeremiah O'Donovan Rossa.

Father was the second youngest of the brothers, but failed to secure a commission in the army, as Mick, his older brother, had done. He was invited to take over the family pottery works, but declined this because business in the town had been devastated when, after the Truce, the British troops pulled out. He studied pharmacy for a time, but with the family coffers now depleted, he had to abandon that too. Given the ferment of the time, however, what he really wanted was to serve the fledgling state, so he joined the army, participated actively in supporting the Dublin Guard when they arrived in the gunboat *The Helga* to take over Youghal town, following the Truce, and then transferred into the Garda Síochána, with the rank of sergeant from the outset.

Father tended to take risks and might have prospered as an entrepreneur. Even though being a risk-taker was not the wisest of dispositions for a garda sergeant, he took them anyway, driven on by his innate impulsiveness. In his very first posting towards the end of the Civil War, he was sent, with three new recruits, to open a new station in County Offaly. Though the force was strictly an unarmed one, when his barracks was threatened with burning he sought advice from Laois-Offaly Garda headquarters in Tullamore as to what he should do. 'Do the best you can, Sergeant' was the reply. It was a reflection of how men chosen for leadership, at that turbulent time, were expected to use their wits and, if they erred, to take the consequences. Father felt that the cryptic reply from headquarters gave him a free hand, so he sandbagged the barracks front and back, borrowed shotguns from the local farmers and waited. In the event, no attack came, but he knew that by using firearms he could have been dismissed from the force if anyone had been hurt. However, he got away with it and tended to make up the rules to suit himself after that.

His loyalty to friends could at times get him into a spot of bother, as happened on the occasion that he allowed Jim Murray, from nearby Oola Garda station, to practice his hammer throwing in the barrack garden at Pallas. With his very first effort, Murray's throw was way off course and crashed through the roof of Dillon's pub. 'You bloody fool; what the hell do you think you're doing?' Father exploded, as he quickly put Murray back on his bicycle and sent him home. He then had to go to Dillon's and stand everyone a drink, not a gesture he was accustomed to making. Fortunately, the missile had lodged in the attic space, but if it had gone further there could have been fatal consequences.

An earlier encounter with Murray—whom he had known in the Garda training depot—was no less painful. When visiting Mother's homestead in County Mayo, Father went one Sunday with his brother-in-law to a football match in nearby Ballindine. The referee failed to show and, though he was a stranger in the town, Father volunteered to take the whistle, only to discover, as the match progressed, that his old friend Murray was playing on the visiting team. The playing pitch was so rough, it was scarcely worthy of the name. At a crucial stage of the match, when the visitors were losing, Murray came up to Father and *sotto voce* said, 'Sarge, give us a free on good ground?' Father duly obliged and Murray's shot sailed over the crossbar to square the match. Their conversation, however, had been overheard and some of the local team quickly realized that there were two policemen on the pitch colluding against them. The upshot was that Father, with his brother-in-law in tow, had to flee cross-country to escape the wrath of the home team's supporters.

Stories of Father's unorthodoxy were legion. He once found a man drunk and disorderly about the village, put him in a cell to sober him up, threw an old policeman's greatcoat over him and left the door unlocked, having shown him where the lavatory was. Shortly afterwards, a familiar figure wearing an old police greatcoat turned up beside him in Cunningham's pub and ordered himself a pint. Father rounded on him at first for daring to abscond. Then, softening, he stood the man a drink before escorting him, still attired in the same greatcoat, to the next bus home.

However, it was not Father but Dan and James Byrne who would bear the full brunt of the land row now looming, Timmy Cronin still refusing to believe that the family land sold to the Kennedys, when his father had died suddenly, was other than a land-grab. Father seemed to have a good relationship with both men nominated for protection duty, although he must have known that they were to some extent at loggerheads with one another, however much they tried to conceal that fact. Yet he had not the heart to discipline them formally, fearing it would damage their future careers. It was a considerable risk to take.

Father saw Dan as the smartest recruit he had ever met. One day soon after he arrived, I heard Mother ask him, 'Jim, how's the new lad getting on?'

'He's gutsy,' Father answered, 'on his toes—a lad I wouldn't mind having beside me in a tight corner.'

There would be many of those in the weeks and months ahead.

CHAPTER 5

Dan Duff would face his sternest test yet at an unlikely venue—a circus. He had come to us in the summer, believing that he had been lucky in his first posting, for he saw Pallas as a tranquil village in a most attractive rural setting. He had not yet learnt that he was earmarked for armed protection night duty and he thought he would have all the time in the world to indulge his passions for writing poetry, sketching some of the local scenery and, when barrack orderly, giving free rein to his magnificent voice in that vast building.

And though, in his early days in Pallas, he did realize that dream briefly, he soon found the reality of life in the village to be very different. For a time at least, he was forced to silence that great voice of his, lay down his pen, put away his crayons and be ready to engage with the toughs of the area. In the process he had to summon up some of the exceptional agility I knew he possessed and find there a means of defending himself and preventing himself from being punched, if not kicked to death. For the Scanlons were coming and one of their hard men, when having a drink in a local pub the week before, had been heard to remark, with not a little venom: 'I can't wait to get my hands on that young bastard who pulled Tom down from the car. When I do, trust me, I'll skin the fucker alive.'

In fact, this drunken fool had given the game away, for Tom Scanlon and his henchmen had already put it brazenly about that they intended to teach the officers of Pallas station a lesson. No one thereafter was fooled by their pretence that they intended to take on the gardaí collectively, for everyone knew then that they were after only one man—the young rookie who had dared them, in a recent incident, to have respect for the law of the land.

It may seem odd that the Scanlons chose the circus to settle a score, but in the small villages of rural Ireland the night of the annual circus had always offered a rare opportunity for those with vengeance in their hearts. For one thing, almost everyone showed up on the night; for another, at the end of the show it was as easy as pie for those seeking revenge for some perceived wrong to stalk their quarry in the rush that usually followed the ending of the circus into the sportsfield outside. There, in the confusion, they could strike swiftly from behind and hope that in the semi-darkness they would not be recognized as they laid their man low, ready you might say for burial.

And so when a rumour swept the village that there was going to be trouble at the upcoming event, most people knew roughly what that meant. Many of the toughs in the area, however, were not all that perturbed and arrived on the night in their droves, rubbing their hands in eager anticipation of an unscheduled confrontation, for them a spectacle far more exciting and enthralling than the antics of clowns and jugglers. These men hung around the entrance that doubled as an exit, or took seats just inside the tent, not sure whether the action would be inside or outside when the last fanfare sounded.

In the old days, the circus arranged its own sideshow to add spice to the event and thus bring the fans along in numbers. As a rule they invited the local toughs to take on the strongmen of the circus, who usually were a formidable bunch of misfits who joined the circus as it toured the country. They usually were more than a match for the local boyos and the guards usually came in force to prevent matters from getting out of hand and were only too delighted when the local toughs took a hiding.

As I sat with my brother Jamie just inside the entrance on circus night, I was dismayed to see Dan enter alone. Only six or seven paces away to the left were Tom Scanlon and four of his men. All were attired in long black overcoats, the badge of the undertaking profession and, to my surprise, they had in tow an attractive, fashionably dressed young woman. They appeared to have consumed some alcohol, no doubt to fortify themselves so that, with all the greater confidence and vigour, they could prosecute the dastardly undertaking on which they were embarked.

And yet, as Dan stood there quietly, he did not appear in the least worried by their presence, his left hand, as usual, resting lightly inside the lapel of his greatcoat, the other thrust casually in the right-hand pocket. I wondered if that calm exterior was really a mask for considerable inner turmoil, for he must have known that a violent attack on him was imminent.

I was dismayed not to see a single colleague in Dan's support. Byrne, I knew, would see little of interest in a circus, while McCabe, under those glaring circus lights, almost certainly would feel his tortured soul laid bare. Hollis was present, but away at the back in civic clothes, clearly ready to scamper at the first sign of trouble.

My sense of relief was palpable, however, when Father finally arrived on the scene, flashlight still on in his huge right hand. It was likely that he would have checked every corner outside with that flashlight before entering the tent, in case additional

Scanlon henchmen were lying in wait. He then stood shoulder to shoulder with his young protégé as they conferred on how to handle the looming confrontation. Jamie and I were worried to see Dan and Father so outnumbered, but suddenly our attention was diverted when, to the strains of 'Blaze Away', the show began dramatically with a troupe of dancing girls erupting into the ring. They performed an array of tricks with joyful abandon, somersaulting and finally forming a human pyramid, almost reaching the tent roof. The applause was tumultuous.

In quick succession there was a clown riding a horse and pretending to loud cheers that he could not hang on; then a juggler, a fire eater and a magician, after which three starved-looking camels wandered in, obviously rather bemused through having strayed far from their natural habitat. Immediately, the dancing troupe surged in once more and the girls began somersaulting over the animals whose mouths were firmly strapped in case, in their hunger, they began snapping at the young nymphs.

The interval came suddenly and one of the most belligerent of Scanlon's men, by the name of Power, rose to go to the makeshift privy outside. As he passed Dan, he lowered his shoulder and jostled him. Dan was about to react when Father nudged him firmly in the ribs. I was within earshot.

'Don't be drawn, boy. They want you to strike first. Stay cool.'

It was, however, an omen for what was to come. On his return, the fellow stopped in front of Dan and, eyeballing him fiercely, muttered an implied threat: 'Are you as good a man tonight as the day you pulled Tom Scanlon down from the car?'

Dan did not answer, but was obviously intent on sticking with the strategy he and Father had agreed on. Father then decided that the best form of defence was attack, of a sort. He strode over to the Scanlon troupe, determination in his every step. Pointing with emphasis to each one of the men in turn, he clearly warned them of the consequences if they made trouble. For a time they appeared subdued, surprised perhaps at the vehemence of his warning.

But tension was mounting now and Jamie and I feared that a violent row would engulf us all. A sudden roll of drums signalled the high-wire act. We watched anxiously as a very beautiful woman faltered halfway across the wire. All was silent save for the roll of the drums. She carried a long pole for balance. When safely across, she whipped up a bicycle as if it was a mere toy and, unsteadily, began cycling across the wire. We could scarcely look. But again, to deafening applause, she made it.

We knew by then that the end game was near. We waited, hardly daring to breathe. Suddenly all eyes were on Father as he summoned over a circus hand. Then the circus manager appeared quickly and conferred with him. He was an impressive, portly man in evening dress, with a magnificent waistcoat and sleek black hair, brilliantined back. He was nodding vigorously, when Father told him what was afoot.

As he moved away, I could just catch their final exchange.

'We want you to leave the lights fully on.'

'Certainly, Sergeant. Anything else?'

'Can you give us more light outside?'

'We'll do what we can, sir.'

The moment of truth had arrived. Lights were suddenly turned on outside. A circus horse with rider in a cowboy outfit galloped into the ring. It was a sign that the show was almost over, for the wretched animal was forced to gallop into the ring to entertain us every time there was a delay in introducing a new act. Father then turned abruptly to his young colleague and, jerking his head towards the exit, gave him a terse command: 'Now skip it, boy, and make space for yourself.'

Dan strode swiftly towards the exit, tightening the strap of his cap around his chin as he went. The Scanlon men were on their feet and after him like a shot out of a gun, but Father blocked their way. Anticipating their headlong dash, he went down like a rugby prop and, with the help of the circus manager, grabbed them by their long black coat-tails, in an endeavour to anchor them to the ground. A fellow named Power broke free immediately and charged outside to find his quarry, hands up in defensive mode, with tons of space in which to manoeuvre.

But Power had no technique, no defence; he just went flailing in on Dan, hoping to overpower him. He took a fierce left jab in the mouth and collapsed to the ground. A second man then came into the attack; he too was out of his depth and was felled by a similar short firm jab to the face. A third very small man hovered while Father and the circus manager held on grimly to the other two. The two grounded men now staggered to their feet as Dan backed away, hands still up, fearing that several men were going to attack him together.

It was then Jamie and I heard some heartening words. A giant of a man beside us, a friend of the barracks, began to remove his watch as he murmured to us: 'I'd better take this off, lads, in case I have to get involved in this thing.'

He was a powerfully built man with enormous fists and his words reassured us. After a moment, however, when it became clear that Dan's defensive skills were keeping the men at bay, he drawled again, as if to himself: 'The fools, the fools. Have they not done their homework on him? Do they not know the lad's a former army boxing champ?'

The hostilities did not last long after that. A little man, a gravedigger, maddened to see his employers bloody and defeated, made one final, desperate attack. He was a veteran of the battle of the Somme, no longer young. Many were the trenches he had dug in his time in France, and many the comrades he had laid to rest there. Some of his taller colleagues had been decapitated by German shells. But the little man from the Somme kept his head in every sense until that night. Dan, so relentless were the attacks on him, was in no mood to differentiate between tall and small, young and old. And so, that left jab of his flashed out once more, the little man's head was rocked backwards and he too was laid low.

The crowd gasped. The young guard should have clinched with the little man and spared him, they said. He should not have used so much violence. Why not arrest these men, they said. Why this? Why that? But in Dan's face that night I did not see anger, aggression, even triumph. What I saw frightened me a little. I saw naked fear.

It had been a long night. But there was still one bizarre twist to come. Dan and Father declined to make arrests. They went instead into the circus tent to offer their thanks to the manager. But when they finally returned to the barracks, there were five men there before them seeking out the superintendent and a doctor. Neither was available. They had already reported, incredibly, that they had suffered at the circus an unprovoked assault by a young guard. Father and Dan made arrests and proffered counter charges. There was resistance; two men, Dillon and Malone, ran for home. All was confusion.

Later, as I lay awake, I wondered what it was about Dan that inspired such affection in some of us who knew him well, and enmity, if not downright hatred, in those who did not. Was it his youthfulness or his refusal to be cowed by a domineering gang? Perhaps it was it that he was a stranger in our midst who wore the uniform of a policeman in respect of which profession some folk still had long and bitter memories, but to my mind it was something altogether deeper. Was it perhaps that heroic spirit we knew him to possess, which emerged in some subliminal form and made lesser men, when in his presence, uneasy, if not hostile?

Before nodding off, I said a prayer and, remembering the agitated crowd, it occurred to me that there was once an infinitely more talented young man who also left His homeland and went among strangers, to serve them and preach to them with only love and kindness in His heart. And they misunderstood and murmured and threatened and, unlike my friend, in His humility and passivity, He declined to defend Himself. And, for His pains, they not only physically attacked Him, they crucified Him.

CHAPTER 6

From the first time I met him I came to believe that Dan may have harboured a secret fear that fate would not be kind to him, and I wondered now if the circus incident could possibly have reinforced that fear and caused him to believe that there was worse to follow. Ill luck had dogged him ever since he had come to Pallas, but he was not a great believer in the notion of luck. On the contrary, he seemed to believe that all things were preordained.

Not surprisingly, therefore, in view of this and the attitude of the local people to his predicament on the night of the circus, he was pessimistic about the outcome of the charge of assault against him in the courts. There were some good reasons why his pessimism may have been justified. For one thing, no one other than Father and I had come forward to give evidence for him, his independence of mind probably inhibiting him from even asking for witnesses.

It was not the wisest of attitudes, however, given the situation in which he found himself, for it left him without a single independent witness to the events on the night of the circus. It may have been, of course, that, even if pressed, the local people would be reluctant to become involved in a confrontation in the courts between the guards and a group of local undertakers.

Since Dan had been confiding in me more and more, though I was three or four years younger than he, I decided, one afternoon, to query him as to how he felt about the matter.

'How do you think it will go?' I asked.

'Difficult to say,' he replied gloomily. 'Their solicitor, apparently, is a tough customer and the brother of an influential local politician.'

'But he can't alter the facts, can he?'

'No, he can't, but with his blustering and aggressive style, they say he rarely loses a case.'

'But surely the district justice will not fall for that?'

'Pat', he declared, somewhat impatiently, 'the district justice is quite old and hard of hearing.'

In the event, Dan's vision of what would happen was not too far wrong, except for one thing. And that one thing was that in the end it was a young woman, exquisitely dressed and devilishly seductive, who would nearly bring him ruin. And how ironic, for here was a young man who, in his short time with us, found that any attractive young women he had met all but fell around the place in their eagerness to be noticed by him, while their mothers vied with one another in insisting that he was just the perfect match for their darling daughters. And yet it was such a young woman who would now all but destroy Dan.

And so to the courts. As luck would have it, our solicitor, Lynam, was to prove ineffective, while Dudley, for the Scanlons, was abrasive and intimidating. We knew immediately that Dan had hired the wrong man.

At 11 a.m. the court clerk entered, and in a ringing tone cried out, 'Silence in court.' There was a hush as the ageing district justice followed as quickly as his advancing years permitted. We all stood; he did likewise for the briefest of moments and then eased himself slowly into his chair. The court, notwithstanding the district justice's weak appearance, was now in formal session. The clerk called out the case to be heard: 'In the matter of Thomas Scanlon suing Garda Dan Duff for alleged assault.'

It was probably a deliberate policy of Dudley's not to permit the other four of the Scanlon group to sue, because he feared they might not stand up well to cross-examination.

It was, of course, logical to hear the plaintiff's case first and Dudley was on his feet in a flash. Peering over his spectacles at the district justice, he said, aggressively, 'I beg leave to call the plaintiff.' The justice nodded wearily and, removing his glasses, rubbed his tired eyes. Dudley, noting the justice's condition, quickly assured him that he would not detain him for long. The justice thanked him. The cunning Dudley had scored over us already by all but suggesting, in his breezy fashion, that the defence case was so flimsy that he expected to demolish it in quick order.

He called Thomas Scanlon to the witness box and invited him to relate what had happened on the night of the circus.

'I went to Pallas to the circus with some friends. On the way I picked up a lady friend. We all went for a drink. I then went to the circus and sat alone with Miss Ryan. When leaving, the guard struck me in the mouth.'

'Did he give any reason?'

'No, my Lord.'

'What happened next?'

'I then went to the barracks and asked to see the superintendent and a doctor. Neither was brought. Then the sergeant and Garda Duff came in and the sergeant arrested me for assaulting the garda. I did not strike Duff. It was he that struck me.'

Questioned by Lynam, Scanlon played a dead bat to everything: he had seen nothing, heard nothing, and done nothing wrong. Lynam's questioning of him made no headway: 'Did you see any of your male friends at the circus?'

'No, sir.'

'Did you see them in grips with the guards?'

'No.'

'Did you jostle the guard or see your friend Power do it?'

'No, I did not.'

'Did you see your friend Power attack Garda Duff?'

'No.'

'Did you yourself attack him when he had beaten off Power's attack?'

'No, I did not.'

As was his prerogative, Dudley called only one other witness, Scanlon's girlfriend, fearful no doubt that if he called his various male friends, they would not have been smart enough to follow the agreed storyline.

Miss Ryan was a joy to behold as she entered the witness box, exquisitely attired, with a ready smile and a plunging neckline. Even when taking the oath, she remained effervescent. It was, presumably, part of the Dudley–Scanlon strategy to present her in as irresistible a light as possible, aiming perhaps to exploit any possible weakness Lynam may have for the more striking members of the fair sex. Before giving evidence, Miss Ryan turned to acknowledge the justice himself, and though it was unlikely that the less than virile-looking law man would be swayed by her winsomeness, you could never tell.

It occurred to me, given the young woman's extraordinary self-assurance, that she could be an actress or a fashion girl or belong to any of a number of allied professions. She gave evidence in a cocksure manner, smiling throughout. She saw, she said, Garda Duff strike her friend but, significantly, she did not say she was at his side at the time. Lynam, however, failed to pursue her on this point. She saw little else, she said, for her friend was bleeding badly from the mouth and she was concerned only to comfort him. She did notice a garda's cap on the ground, but did not know how it had got there.

As he addressed her, it was not surprising that Lynam appeared distracted, for Miss Ryan's overt seductiveness was breathtaking. If it was a deliberate piece of role-playing under Dudley's masterly eye, then she was performing brilliantly.

Lynam tried, feebly, to probe her evidence for possible implausibility, but she dealt with him effortlessly.

'Whose cap was it the sergeant picked up off the ground, and how did it get there?'

'I can only assume, sir, that it fell off the guard when he rushed at my friend and struck him.'

'I see. And what would you say was the reason why the guard, as you allege, struck Mr Scanlon?'

She did not answer this question, at least not in verbal form, but instead threw her arms out wide, in mock mystification, revealing all the more prominently her multiple physical charms, as if to say, but not quite saying it, 'Jealousy, I suppose.'

It was, of course, well known that Miss Ryan was a much sought after young woman. She appeared, however, to have deliberately left the impression in court that Dan Duff, who was depending on the outcome of this case perhaps for his very livelihood, was one of a vast band of her jilted lovers.

I knew this to be untrue and a foul slur on Dan, especially

given that it was calculated to undermine his case and perhaps ruin him. Dudley and his clients knew full well that the question of the absence of motive for the alleged assault was the crucial weakness in their case and this crafty young adventuress had now falsely and wickedly supplied it, as if she was well used to finding the green-eyed monster rife among her competing lovers.

Unusually for him, Dudley managed a smile, which could only mean that he sensed triumph for, amazingly, Lynam had failed to raise the merest doubt about Miss Ryan's credibility. He, Dudley, then informed the justice that he had other men in court, but proposed not to call them for they had been summoned, he emphasized, to appear at another court on a charge of assaulting the guards, and on this account he said, 'it would be unfair to leave them open to questioning'. He knew well that he dared not call them, for these men were not bright and might have let the side down. Incredibly, Lynam raised no objection to this ploy.

The case for the defence was then heard. Lynam invited Dan to take the stand. He spoke in a clear voice, happily with no sign of nerves. He had been standing, he said, inside the entrance on the night of the circus and had been jostled twice by a man he later identified as Power, who had been sitting at the performance with the plaintiff. Power had asked him aggressively if he was as good a man as when he had pulled Tom Scanlon down from the cart. Power, he insisted, had used bad language and wanted to fight and when Dan was leaving the circus, Power assaulted him.

Then, he went on, the plaintiff struck him and he hit back in self-defence. The same man then struck him a second time and another man named Kelly assaulted him. He emphasized, however, that he did no more than defend himself, and that it was untrue to say that he had struck the Scanlon boss first.

Dudley then cross-examined Dan. Cleverly, he avoided questioning him on the incident at the circus and focused on the events in the barracks, where he knew the guards were taken by surprise and therefore were on weaker ground. He then forcefully challenged the young defendant: 'Are you saying that my client is telling lies?'

'His evidence is an absolute perjury.'

'Do you say that he went voluntarily to the barracks after beating up the guards? Surely you don't expect the court to believe that?'

'He wanted to get his speak in first.'

'Why did you not call the superintendent for him?'

'It was too late.'

'I put it to you that neither the sergeant nor you wanted to produce the superintendent.'

'No.'

Father then corroborated Dan's evidence, but Dudley, in questioning him, was dismissive.

'Do you say you did not know where the superintendent was?'

'Yes.'

'Why did you not arrest Dillon and Malone?'

'They had run for home.'

'Why did you leave it as late as last Saturday to issue a summons to them?'

'There was a lot of preparatory work to be done.'

'I'd want to be a bit of a fool to accept that.'

'That's the truth.'

'Is it, Sergeant? I put it to you that you and Duff concocted your evidence in order to prevent Duff being put through the hoop by his own authorities.'

'We did not.'

Dudley, sensing triumph once more, was cock-a-hoop, sarcastic almost, as he rounded on me when I entered the witness box.

'To whom did you make your statement?'

'To Garda Duff.'

'I see. Are the words in your statement yours or his?'

'The sense is mine, sir, but he helped me with some of the words.'

'He helped you with the words, did he? The defendant in this case actually phrased your statement? My young man, that makes your testimony to my mind next to useless. That will be all.'

I returned to my position red-faced, aware that my statement, far from assisting my friend, had probably injured him. The justice then, as if finally convinced by Dudley's dismissal of my evidence, began in his halting way to deliver his verdict.

'It is, I have to say, a very unpleasant case. I have known Sergeant Kelleher for a long time and hold him in regard. But the plaintiff has told me a story I believe; this makes the other stories appear untrue, but I cannot help that. I, therefore, on the evidence, hold for the plaintiff.'

It was painful in the extreme to be branded a liar in a court of law. When we were filing out silently, I was sure my father and Dan felt the same. Father's face was red with anger as he led the way without waiting to talk to Lynam. Dan was pale and impassive; he seemed too stunned to speak when we reached the car. He had come into the force to see justice done, an idealist, probably believing that once you had judges, courts, lawyers and policemen, the world would be a fairer place. He looked a very disillusioned man that afternoon.

When we were driving home, Father tried to make Dan less despondent. 'Have no fear, boy,' he said; 'we'll have a judge in the Circuit Court for the appeal. We'll dump Lynam and, trust me, we'll overturn this thing. It's a travesty.'

Dan was visibly uplifted by these words and we drove in silence for a time. Before alighting from the car at the barracks, however, Father, given to hyperbole, delivered one final salvo.

'Justice, fellows,' he said, 'is a rare, fragile and elusive thing, and politicians, churchmen and sundry bureaucrats up and down the country would not recognize it if it jumped up and hit them in the face. But justice will be done the next day, for if I have to go to Mexico myself for him, I'll have the circus manager here for the appeal.'

Angry words they may have been, but they were the sweetest we had heard all day.

CHAPTER 7

That woman! She was the first person to catch the eye when we entered the courtroom on the day of the appeal. Her hair was more beautifully coiffed, her skirt tighter, her elegantly clad model's legs crossed for all to see. She seemed once again to regard herself as the centre of attention and the key witness, whose evidence would decide my young friend's appeal.

But, alas, she was mistaken. For on that second day, some three months later in Limerick District Court, confidently sat a well built middle-aged man in a magnificent dark-striped suit, multi-patterned waistcoat and shining black patent shoes with buckles. Rejoicing in the rather alien-sounding name of Laurence Arthur McDonald, he looked every inch a circus manager. He had been the man in charge on that fateful night and if anyone on earth knew the truth of what had happened, surely, we hoped and believed, it was he.

All eyes were on him from the moment he first entered the courtroom in his flamboyant garb and most knew instinctively who he was and that his presence surely spelt trouble, not only for the Scanlon boss, but for his entire entourage. Moreover, they knew in their hearts that by the time the circus manager had given his evidence, the ever-alluring Miss Ryan would wish for the ground to open up and swallow her.

Yet despite her previous attempts to undermine and even destroy my good friend, to my shame I found that the young woman fascinated and intrigued me, her shamelessness, her ever-flirtatious smile, her raw sexual power that seemed to make the strongest men salivate with desire. And I knew that by the time the day's proceedings were ended, however much her magnetism may have softened us towards her, she would have been seen more completely for what she was—not only a femme fatale, but a consummate actress.

As I studied her, it occurred to me that she was a trophy of sorts for the Scanlon men, whom they had won against stiff opposition and who accompanied them everywhere, except to their funerals. In truth, given that they spent most of their days tramping gloomy ancient graveyards, they needed her, if only as a therapy, to soothe, comfort and make merry with them when all the prayers were done and the last shovelfuls of earth scattered on some poor innocent's grave.

The atmosphere was tenser than the almost casual ambience of the earlier court. Contributing to this greater air of seriousness were certain key changes in personnel. The judge on the bench was of an infinitely sterner disposition than the hapless septuagenarian of the Limerick Civil Court. And, on our side, there was a new legal man, Thomas Stanley, tall and authoritative, who took the place of the dandified and ineffectual Lynam. We knew that Stanley would prove a match for the bullyboy, Dudley, who had masterminded the villainous Scanlon triumph that first day and who was still representing Scanlon.

But it was only when the circus manager rose from his seat when called to give evidence that the fairly full courtroom hummed with expectation and, no doubt, for the Scanlon side, with apprehension. The murmuring soon grew louder and, pounding the bench forcefully with his gavel, the judge cried out 'Silence in court'. The sartorially impeccable former lion-tamer then stepped confidently into the witness box. By my side Dan seemed ice-cool, already apprised of the substance of McDonald's testimony.

Mr Stanley promptly addressed the witness when he had taken the oath.

'Tell us, Mr McDonald, what you saw on the night of July twenty-third.'

The circus manager replied in a clear voice with an unmistakable English inflection.

'I noticed a scuffle just outside the circus tent when the performance ended. I expected it, for the sergeant had told me at the interval that he believed his young colleague was about to be attacked. I saw a man, whom I later identified as Mr Power, without apparent provocation pursue and strike Garda Duff. Then I saw another man, whom I understand to be Mr Scanlon, lunge aggressively at the officer. I was extremely concerned for the young garda's safety and I rushed to help the sergeant hold back the second man. Then a third man, a little fellow, dashed at Garda Duff after he had beaten off the other two. I picked up the young guard's cap and advised him and the sergeant to remain in the tent for safety. I told Power, who was hanging around the entrance, to move off. He replied aggressively: 'If you don't mind your own business, you will get the same.'

There was a gasp around the courtroom, for McDonald's clear and unambiguous statement had a greater ring of truth than any other. He had, of course, no ulterior agenda and, at a stroke, had all but buried the Scanlon men.

The judge, however, seemingly in dismay at the appalling conflict in the sworn evidence confronting him, passed a hand wearily over his brow. He invited Dudley to respond, but the lawyer's appetite for the cause had already evaporated. He had but one question for the witness that he posed rather waspishly. 'How can you possibly be sure of the identity of the men you saw attack the garda?'

A flicker of a smile crossed the circus man's face before he replied, 'Of course I know who they are; they were around the tent long enough for the sergeant to name them for me, one by one.'

The judge then recalled to the witness box not, mark you, Mr Scanlon, but the cocksure Miss Ryan, acknowledging implicitly that the case came down, in the end, to her word against Mr McDonald's. He read to her the evidence she had given at the earlier court and asked her, sternly, if she could reconcile this with McDonald's evidence. We discovered, to our surprise, that the lady was human after all. Tears began to flow, as did her ample mascara. She made unconvincing dramatic gestures with her slender hands, as she struggled to reply: 'I was on my knees, for God's sake, attending to my friend's bloody face! How could I see what else was going on?'

She looked around in search of a friendly face. There was none. Hard men are not impressed by emotional outbursts, and women, used and abused by them, are quickly abandoned once they have served their purpose. Miss Ryan looked more alone than possibly she had ever been, while the Scanlon boss, seeming utterly unmoved, stared straight ahead of him. She wept copiously into her handkerchief while, ominously, Dudley, her one-time champion, was silent. To my eye, however, she remained an irresistible young woman who probably had been coerced into partaking in this dastardly enterprise. My heart went out to her.

But the Scanlon race was now run and this judge did not hang about when the truth was staring him straight in the face.

'I have two very contradictory accounts of what happened. It's quite clear that Garda Duff gave Scanlon a more effective beating than the latter gave him. But, surprisingly, while the dispute took place in full view of the villagers of Pallas, none of them was witness in the case. I cannot see why the respondent could not get independent testimony. I am, therefore, not satisfied with the evidence disclosed. Accordingly, I am reversing the decision of the district justice.'

He pounded the bench with his gavel, even more vehemently than before, reflecting perhaps his anger at the aplomb with which perjury, before his very eyes, had been committed.

The judge had hardly left his seat when, defeat written all over their faces, some of the Scanlon hangers-on slipped quickly out of court. It was clear there would be no merry-making in Scanlon country that night.

As we left the courtroom, we were more relieved than jubilant. Dan had escaped defeat, and possibly summary dismissal from the force, by the skin of his teeth. I noted how silent, reflective and impassive he was, puzzled as to how he could have come so close to defeat. I could not help being impressed, however, by his calm and undemonstrative demeanour, but I wondered what, under the mask, the entire affair had done to his inner self. He was not a man to show frustration easily, unless he was pushed to the very limit of his endurance. When that happened, as we saw on the night of the circus, the consequences for his tormentors could be lethal, for foolhardy is the man who finally arouses a basically gentle, passive soul.

He had now seen off the Scanlon men and could only hope

they would not trouble him again. Undoubtedly the episode had left its mark. And he knew, as we all did, that it was as nothing to the test of his mettle to come. For, when shortly he would march out on armed night duty in the land row, he would have to partner James Byrne, a man who, to say the least, disliked him and, moreover, he had to be prepared, at every moment, to confront an angry land agitator, Timmy Cronin, if he showed up some night armed, as was very possible.

When we left the court, however, Christy Connor, our ever-thirsty driver, looked as if he expected the celebrations to be immediate. Chuckling delightedly as he puffed on yet another cigarette, Christy addressed Father with the words, 'After you, Skipper,' assuming that the sergeant would lead us to the nearest public house. A former seafaring man, in his mind's eye Connor saw Father as commanding the little village as if it were a great ship at sea and addressed him accordingly. Father never took offence, but on that afternoon, looking our driver firmly in the eye, told him, 'Christy, we're going home.' Celebrations could wait but, in the event, not for long.

Father's association with Connor went back a long way. He always sat very close to him as the latter drove, one protective arm around his shoulders, their heads all but touching. And those of us sitting in the rear never knew if their whispered conversations were initiated by Father to keep his always slightly inebriated driver awake and alert to the potholes in the road or if, instead, they were intended to extract information from him about local people, in trouble of one sort or another. At the very least, Father would have found those journeys an excellent opportunity to hear from Christy the latest salacious gossip, for few knew as much about what went on in the locality. And since Father gave him more driving assignments than anyone else, Connor returned the compliment freely and would not have dared deny Father anything of interest that he might have overheard on his travels.

CHAPTER 8

It was late in the evening of the court proceedings when, looking out from an upstairs window of the barracks, I observed three men moving like shadows in the darkness towards Cunningham's public house. Only because a chink of light leaped out as they entered the pub did I identify them. It occurred to me what an extraordinary group they were—each an artist of a sort, capable through his originality and wit of enlivening any social gathering, especially of drinking men.

While Father's storytelling tended to dominate these occasions, Dan's singing was a new feature, but it was hackney man Christy Connor who was the wisecracking genius of the threesome. Not so much in the pub, but after closing hours, he held court, especially on summer nights, under the road signs at the crossroads. His audience were mostly penniless young farming men and World War II veterans with broken bodies, bachelors all, as was Connor himself. His shafts of wit were directed at the more pompous in village society, the shopkeepers and pub-owners who, to paraphrase Yeats, fumbled grim-faced in their greasy tills and tended to despise the impecunious and those down on their luck.

As Connor relentlessly poked fun at their failings, his audience laughed all the louder, for they themselves could rarely afford to cross the threshold of pubs, let alone join in the more serious drinking sessions in Cunningham's.

But it was my friend, Dan, who stole the show in Cunningham's that night, for as I strolled out to the village near closing time I was stopped in my tracks on hearing from the pub a tenor voice the like of which, I had never heard live before. It could have been John McCormack himself.

I drew close and peered through a gap in the heavy curtain. It was indeed Dan in characteristic pose, his left hand resting lightly inside the lapel of his greatcoat. As he finished, the exclusively male clientele stood in awe, some with their glasses halted halfway to their lips so wonderfully had he rendered that song. Behind the bar a dark, attractive young Kerry girl watched Dan intently, half-smiling, half in tears, enchanted. To those present, he may have been viewed before as a strange, solitary and reflective youth, but that night he was a revelation. They applauded as he finished, their glasses clinking merrily again and their animated conversation and laughter resuming. It was a party that endured well into the night.

Not qualified to join the happy gathering, I drifted away to re-enter the old barracks by the back yard, for the front door was always securely locked on the stroke of midnight. As I went, that first verse, so wonderfully sung, still haunted me:

> *I hear you calling me.*
> *You called me when the moon had veiled her light,*
> *Before I went from you into the night;*
> *I came—do you remember?—back to you*
> *For one last kiss beneath the kind stars' light.*

Knowing what Dan had endured ever since he had come to Pallas, and struck by the depth of feeling he had put into that song, I could not help thinking it was from him a cry for help of sorts, for someone, a woman perhaps, to console him. Some gut feeling told me that if he was detailed, as seemed likely, for armed protection duty in the company of the fractious James Byrne, it could prove a disastrous pairing, a partnership, you might say, from hell.

And so I was already in sombre mood as I crossed the grim, enclosed barrack yard. It was in utter darkness, the gravel crunching under my feet the only sound. The monstrous old building loomed over me and memories came flooding back of some of the horrific things I had seen there as a boy, one so weird that it made my flesh creep. I believed then, as if it were gospel, that men who died violently, unprepared, remained forever wilful, restless spirits and often walked abroad on certain nights. But it was two incidents that I had seen much earlier that conditioned me to fear, all the more, that something similar would happen in the barrack yard again.

One of these concerned, an army captain a friend of Father's, who had come to visit him one Christmas Day. He went to the river to poach some salmon for our table. He was alone and was using gelignite, the shock of which alone, he knew, would kill the fish. Most tragically, he slipped in with the explosive and blew himself away. What they could find of him they brought into the yard covered with a white sheet. I looked on, frozen with fear.

Soon after this tragedy, an old truck, laden with heavy scrap iron, drove into the village at speed. The driver struggled to take the bend downhill at Cunningham's; he failed and the truck capsized, pinning him beneath, against a wall. There was little hope for him, for lifting equipment took ages to come from Limerick. The villagers kept a prayer vigil all day beside the debris, saying to the driver, repeatedly, Acts of Contrition. I looked on terrified. The man's body was later laid out in the yard.

And so, for long after, I avoided that space after dark. But one wild winter's night we ran short of milk for breakfast and Mother sent my little sister, Esther, with me to fetch some at Dillon's shop farther down the street. It was very late when, huddled together, we chanced across the yard, our heads covered with our coats, for the rain was driving into our faces and the wind howling around us. We made it safely out of the great wooden gate. Across the road, a line of chestnut trees swayed in the wind and to our side the high prison-like barrack wall, rising above us, hemmed us in. It was by far the darkest part of the street, with only a glimmer of light from Cunningham's, some distance away. On our way back, the wind seemed to rise and the trees to sway more violently as we neared the gate. It was then that it appeared, quite suddenly. A tall weird shadowy figure swept across our path and in the gate before us. It had a long thin face which, in the rain, gleamed like the blade of a scythe. It turned to us with an evil, death-like stare as if daring us to follow it. We still hoped that it might be a very tall man in some strange rain gear going into the barracks by the back entrance. We followed nervously. It had vanished! There was not a soul to be seen, not even a sound on the gravel. I looked quickly behind the gate. There was no one there. It was only then that Esther spoke. Her voice was trembling

'Did you see something too?'

'Yes, I saw a tall figure going in before us.'

'I saw it too,' she replied, now scarcely audible.

With that we fled up the yard, fearing every second that we would be grabbed from behind. The great gaping windows of the barracks were unlit and, therefore, offered no comfort, looking more like giant black holes going back to the end of the universe.

I carried the milk in an open can, but only a half of it survived our panicked dash for safety. We shivered as we entered our quarters, but Mother, Father and one of my younger brothers only laughed at us, telling us that the tall chestnut trees, in a gale, always threw long, seemingly moving, shadows. But Esther and I, comparing notes, agreed on every last detail about what we had seen, and it was not, most definitely not, a chestnut tree uprooting suddenly and, transformed into a ghostly thing, moving swiftly across the street. Yet we told them so. And still they laughed.

A few days later I told Dan that story. It was late one afternoon in the gloomy yard, as he was struggling to repair a puncture on his old bicycle. I had never before seen him with muddied hands.

'Why not take it down to Frank?' I asked.

'Who's Frank?'

'He has a repair shop down by the river. He's only four foot tall and has no hands, but he can fix a puncture in a jiffy.'

'Extraordinary, I'd like to meet him sometime.'

'You'd enjoy watching him. He has a massive head and a face like a great Roman general and you would see immediately that it was from there his genius came.'

'Extraordinary,' he repeated, not quite concentrating, and soon I learnt why.

'In the meantime', I suggested, 'you could borrow mine.'

'That's my problem,' he answered, looking embarrassed. 'I borrowed James's without asking him and he didn't speak to me for four days.'

I had heard, but it was the first time he had mentioned it to me. Clearly it had hurt. He quickly saw that, in the face of his disclosure, I was stuck for words and he changed the subject abruptly: 'Have you ever seen anything here?' he asked, the gloom of the grim yard clearly affecting his mood.

'What do you mean?' I replied evasively, wondering who had told him.

'Have you ever seen anything strange here?'

It was obvious that he had heard about my weird experience and so I told him what I had seen. He hung on my every word, stopping work on his bicycle as he knelt there. When I had finished, he said, 'It's a good story. You should write it down.'

I was pleased. I noticed how his shadowed face made him seem even more handsome and in an odd way more vulnerable too. I felt sorry for him as he finally put the bicycle up against the wall and rubbed his grubby hands together with some distaste. It occurred to me that maybe it would be his story I would write down one day, when his ordeal in Pallas was finally over. I knew even then that it could be a compelling story.

CHAPTER 9

I was soon to have an experience that gave me some little insight into what Dan had suffered already, though I knew it was as nothing compared to what would face him after Christmas. I wanted to be supportive, especially since that he had begun to confide in me more and more about his fears for the future, though never explicitly. Father, however, had other plans for me.

Several months before, he had urged me to join the Local Defence Force, believing that some service would give me a fighting chance of eventually securing a state job, and that it would toughen me for life, something, he believed, I badly needed. Signing on, however, involved going on a month-long army-style training course at two locations, one on the south coast, the other on the west coast. Father was ever watchful in case I found an excuse to opt out, especially on the day the army lorry came to collect the members of our local unit.

I was in the process of donning my uniform in my musty-smelling room on the top floor of the barracks when Father's loud voice reached me.

'Pat, the lorry is here. You'd better get a move on.'

'Yes, coming,' I answered, angry at his tone.

'They'll put you in the clink if you don't hurry.'

Soon I was clattering down the barrack stairs, the hairy collar of

my uniform chafing at my neck and the heavy army boots already
hurting my tender feet. To make matters worse, I was carrying
a Lee Enfield army rifle, a weapon I came to detest. Rifles had
been given to us with advice on how to clean and oil them, the
instructor joking that the Lee Enfield's most important part was
its firing mechanism, the equivalent in a rifle, he said, of a man's
genitalia, and both useless without it. There were loud guffaws at
the comment but, in no humour for joking, I remained stony-
faced. I knew at that early stage that I was not cut out for soldiering,
or for the false camaraderie that went with it.

However, I had no option but to join the six strapping fellows
outside the barracks, leaping like stags in and out of the lorry
while I, red of face, all but fell into the vehicle, my rifle clattering
to the floor. It was not an auspicious start to my brief army
'career'. And, if my self-esteem was already at a low ebb, it hit
rock bottom when I heard the name of the fellow in charge of
our unit. Addressed as 'Smiler' by the others, he was the younger
brother of the Scanlon undertakers, his nickname earned by the
deadly seriousness of his expression at all times. Soon I noted
him regarding me with a beady eye and knew I was in for a
tough time in the weeks to follow.

We spent the first night in an army barracks in Limerick,
virtually without sleep, for most of the unit, as if just released from
a mental institution, spent the night jumping over their rifles while
holding the weapons in front of them, one hand at each end. Those
exhausted from this activity found it hilarious to urinate through
little holes in the floorboards on to the rival unit underneath. The
following morning, after a hasty breakfast that ended with many
throwing rotten eggs at one another, we had to march around the
city in the searing heat to commemorate some ancient battle.

It was during this march that Smiler harried me at every opportunity, and I began to get an understanding of what it must be like for Dan when Byrne constantly needled him. Smiler took advantage of my inexperience as a mere recruit, and it was only years later that I learnt that, in most workplaces, it was recruits who suffered most at the hands of bullies like Byrne and Smiler.

I had had a slight brush with polio as a boy of about twelve and my right hip muscles were weakened, but it showed up in my gait only when I was tired. And so, as I marched, Smiler roared at me every so often, 'Pick it up, Kelleher. Pick it up, man, and stop dragging your feet.' I was thoroughly embarrassed that my secret affliction had been spotted, and I was later to learn that I would not be allowed to parade for prize-giving, Smiler believing that I would endanger the chances of the entire unit winning a prize. I felt it absurd that I was deemed fit enough to enlist in the force to provide cannon fodder for some putative enemy one day, but not fit enough for the beauty parade aspect of army camp. And so I was to spend long periods under canvas, reading the volume Dan had lent me, ironically entitled *Les Miserables*. Dan never said much about his time in the army and I wondered afterwards if, in choosing that book for me, he too had found the experience harrowing.

We left the town of Youghal, County Cork, where in the course of firing range practice it was discovered that I was short-sighted and I suffered the humiliation of being ordered off the range before I did someone an injury. Soon after, we travelled to the seaside town of Lahinch in County Clare. It had rained relentlessly in Youghal and the deluge continued in Lahinch. As we lay on our bellies, on what had once been a golf course, we were invited to imagine that enemy tanks would shortly come over the hill. We had not been issued with waterproof groundsheets and soon were soaked to the skin. But whether war was real or imagined, rain or no rain, the pretence had to go on. We moved up the golf course on our stomachs, snake-like. I had never felt so absurdly preoccupied before in my life. I had been told before joining up that, effectively, army camp would be a paid holiday and that, with any luck, I would find myself in the embrace of some of the beautiful girls of County Clare. In the event, I was to embrace nothing more animated than the cold wet steel of my Lee Enfield.

On my very first evening in Clare my brief period of active service came to an abrupt end. I was not long back in my Nissen hut billet when I discovered that not only was my voice gone, but that I was breathing with great difficulty. The medical people were summoned and seemed alarmed. I was swept away in the night by ambulance to Collins military barracks hospital in Cork, and given a bed in a vast ward containing only three patients. Miraculously, on arrival, my illness disappeared as quickly as it had come. I could only conclude that its source was psychological and, since it was not therefore visible, my physical body took responsibility, so that I would be given treatment.

But the story of my brief army service did not end there. A buxom young nurse came round each day to check my temperature and pulse. Given her charms, it was hardly surprising that my pulse began to race when she appeared. And so I was detained for several weeks and often wondered afterwards if the young lady had been especially chosen to have just that impact on her patients, so as to justify our continuing presence, thus keeping the hospital fully operational, even though, with the war now over, army numbers were in decline.

In the event, my hospital stay proved to be a holiday. A handsome giant and sporting hero of mine, John Cronin, was paymaster, and delivered each week an army private's pay packet and, each evening, two bottles of stout to every patient. But Father's intervention, at some point, was inevitable. He telephoned his brother, an army officer on the reserve, who knew the hospital's medical officer. My release was immediately authorized, my uncle coming to my bedside himself to impart the news. So ingrained in him were the ways of the army that he all but goose-stepped to my bedside and saluted. I shrank in my bed in embarrassment, for this man had an extraordinary record. During the Troubles he had been on several hunger strikes in British jails and with some colleagues had endeavoured to wreck Spike Island Prison, off the Cork coast, when once imprisoned there circa 1920. I felt I had let down the family record.

As I travelled home on the train, I found myself reflecting on the source of my genes, for not only had Father and his brothers been tough and dogged campaigners in the Troubles, but Mother's father and his three brothers were successful adventurers in the Klondike gold rush in 1897, managing to return despite the many hazards along the way, rich enough to buy farms in County Mayo where they had grown up. Their story was never told, for in due course they married and fathered mainly girls, some of whom decided when they reached adulthood, and went in search of 'suitable' husbands, that the constant talk of the less than respectable manner by which their fathers had made their money—by digging it up from the Yukon river in conditions which were sometimes fifty degrees below zero—was not likely to further the girls' marital ambitions.

Mother, in later years, gave me an example of how sensitive

the subject of The Klondike became on social occasions. She was driving, she said, to a reception in County Tipperary to the wedding of one of her Uncle Jack's girls. Her father and Jack occupied the rear seat while Tess, a sister of the bride, drove the car, with Mother by her side. When they neared the venue for the wedding, Tess, on hearing the topic being discussed by the two gold-mining veterans in the rear, stopped the car and turning around, gave the men a stern warning. 'Now, gentlemen', she said, 'if I hear another word today about the Klondike, you can drive yourselves home.' When Mother told me this story, it reminded me of my summer holidays as a teenager in my maternal grandfather's farm in Mayo. For when he and I would walk the fields together in the late evenings, the then ageing giant, his head bowed and his hands behind his back, would lapse into silence and I always sensed that he ached to tell me, the first grandson he would have known, something of his early years, but he could not. His lips were sealed.

The plan to suppress the Klondike story worked particularly well, however, for another of Jack's girls, Delia, who met her husband, Tom Kiernan, at University College Galway. In due course Kiernan was appointed an Irish ambassador abroad and over time served in a number of capitals around the globe. When they married, Delia was already a noted singer of Irish traditional songs and became a great asset to her husband, not merely as a wife, but also as an entertainer on the diplomatic circuit. Moreover, when posted in Rome during World War II, at great risk to her husband and herself, she helped Allied soldiers and Jews escape from the Nazis through the embassy gardens. However, there was a sorrowful side to Delia's fame and achievement, for surveys later showed that ambassadors' wives were at the top of the list of those succumbing to the dreaded disease of alcoholism and, sadly, Delia herself eventually was to become a victim.

And so when, disappointed with my stint in army camp, I asked Mother to tell me which side of our family I was taken after, she said that her mother's people were a milder breed than her father's people, the Murphys. The former were, she said, prim and proper priests and schoolteachers who, as she put it, 'would not say boo to a goose'. One of their number, she told me, was a priest in America and when he came back to Ireland on holiday he drank the best part of a bottle of whiskey a day to cope with his shyness and timidity. They were not the stuff of which soldiers and adventurers were made, but the breed, it seemed, to which I belonged.

On returning home from army camp, I discovered that Father had not revealed to anyone my misadventure and so, although I had failed to win a single star for my efforts there, or even to complete the course, a few of the villagers came out to their front doors to cheer me. As I strode up the village from the railway station, looking lean and tanned, many were approving, one lady gushingly saying to me, 'While we have young men like you, prepared to defend us, the country is in safe hands.' The village butcher, a friend of Father's, winked at me, saying, 'A chip off the auld block, eh!' Father would not have been amused.

When I ran into Dan, I confided in him the truth of my army-camp experience, and my ordeal at the hands of the youngest of the Scanlon men. He smiled ruefully, saying, 'We won't be troubled by that lot again.' Dan knew that it was Father who had urged me to get involved in the Local Defence Force. His own father had been an army sergeant-major and I had presumed that this was how Dan had come to join the army before transferring to the Garda Síochána in the early 1940s. Fathers are well-intentioned, but some are inclined to want their sons to be copies of themselves.

My test, however, was behind me. I had survived, if only just. But Dan's greatest test was yet to come. That was what was on my mind when I asked him about developments in the land row.

'Any sign of a settlement at Mount Catherine?' I asked tentatively.

'No, Pat, I'm afraid it's a stalemate.' He looked pessimistic.

'So you'll be stuck with it…the night duty, I mean?'

'I guess so. I'll just have to make the best of it.'

Sometimes Dan's words concealed more than they revealed about his state of mind, his anxiety often hidden by his exceptional personal charm. His good humour, however, which had bordered on the infectious when he had first come to the barracks, was now less striking.

But the villagers did not quite share his pessimism. With the season of goodwill beckoning, they hoped that, at such a holy time of year the Kennedys and the Cronins, about to confront one another finally at Mount Catherine over the land in dispute, would take a step back from the abyss and forge an eleventh-hour compromise. In the event, that did not come to pass, but the run-up to Christmas was dominated by something else altogether—a golden opportunity for Dan which, if he could only have grasped it, could have changed everything for him for the better.

CHAPTER 10

Poets are said to die young, but they also fall in love faster than most ordinary mortals. And that, on the cusp of Christmas, is precisely what happened to Dan Duff. 'I hear you calling me', he had sung, so plaintively on that night of celebration in Cunningham's. Had his cry been answered? And would he capitalize on his good fortune? To do so, he would have to put aside his fear that fate's cards were stacked against him, and act decisively. Could he?

These were the thoughts that went through my mind one afternoon as together, from the day room window of the barracks, we observed an extraordinary sight, a piece of theatre. Across the street, an eccentric former army colonel (as I learnt) was moving—with his family—into an old stone dwelling, formerly a schoolhouse, set in trees under the shadow of the old Church of Ireland building. The colonel and a truck driver were having an altercation over where precisely a gigantic consignment of turf should be set down, and there was no sign of a resolution, with the former army man gesticulating wildly and stamping up and down, and the wretched truck driver looking more and more harassed.

However, it was not the resolution of this bizarre episode that we awaited eagerly, but the emergence, once more, of a young woman who—before the removal van that had accompanied the truck had driven off—had appeared briefly to help shepherd into the building, with great care, no less a piece of furniture than a grand piano. It was for us an extraordinary stroke of good luck, given the state of affairs in the village, for young men to witness, right opposite the barracks, as ravishing a young woman as either of us had ever seen actually taking up residence across the street. There was no convent school in Pallas and therefore no young women. It was as simple and as stark as that. But, then, neither was there a youth centre, a cinema, or a functioning place of worship, for the old Church of Ireland building was open for a only couple of hours on Sundays, with few worshippers attending. And so, however much we deluded ourselves to the contrary, the village was little more than a crossroads, a staging post, with a monstrous police barracks perched on a hill at one end, looking down threateningly on the villagers and, at the other end, a railway station that took young people away, but rarely brought them back.

True, in some tiny outlying hamlets there were ancient communities, and there were young people still, and one or two of the brighter young women, who had escaped being despatched to convents elsewhere, flashed through Pallas each morning and afternoon on their bicycles, on the way to the Mercy Convent in the village of Doon, at the foot of the Slieve Phelim hills. But they rarely dismounted. It was as if the place was a leper colony and they feared that the briefest of halts would bring upon them some dreadful malady. In truth, they probably sensed an aloofness and latent hostility there. For the village was peopled almost exclusively by an odd assortment of middle-aged policemen and grim-faced pub owners, parasites all, the majority of whom had blown in with the army of occupation in earlier decades and did not really belong in Pallas at all.

And, so, was it any wonder that we watched patiently for one more glance of this young woman, before darkness fell and we mounted that gloomy stairway to our dimly lit and Spartan rooms and, in our fantasies, took her with us to lie together, all the while protecting her beautiful lithe body from the cold steel frames of our state-issue beds in which nightly we moved back and forth in search of sleep. The days were dull, the nights a torture, and oh! how she could have changed that.

But soon, awakened from our happy reveries, we noted that the confrontation across the street had come to an abrupt conclusion. For, in final frustration, the truck driver had decided to dump his cargo unceremoniously, half on the footpath, half on the roadway. And then, as he jumped into his cab and departed in high dudgeon, with the colonel hurling expletives in his wake, there was a new twist.

Father, ever alert to anything that might require his presence, had heard the war of words outside his living room window, and soon bustled onto the street. With his bull-like frame, he confronted the ageing colonel, who backed away from him, as if he was about to be bitten by an Alsatian.

'What's going on here?' Father asked the colonel aggressively.

'Sorry, Sergeant. We'll move it in as quickly as possible,' the colonel answered sheepishly.

'You'd better. It's a danger to traffic. Where have you come from?'

But Father's bark was always worse than his bite and when the colonel introduced himself and appeared contrite, they were soon friends. Father then took up a point-duty man's stance to allow a donkey and cart to pass by, the only serious traffic at that late hour of the autumn afternoon.

His point was well made, however, for with darkness threatening, even the humble pedestrian was at risk, unless the roadway was cleared forthwith. And so the colonel and Father, as new friends and neighbours, joined forces: Father promptly waylaid some youths passing on bicycles who, with the promise of a few shillings from the colonel, parked their bikes swiftly against the wall, and began pitching the stuff, sod for sod, into the colonel's front garden. Observing with satisfaction how effectively the youths were making inroads into the encroaching pile, the two men dusted off their hands and departed to Cunningham's, the final destination in the village, as a rule, for men who have resolved a difficult problem and now wished to drink to it.

And then finally she emerged again. She stepped out down the pathway with an elegant stride, picking her way carefully through the lumps of turf. She smiled charmingly at the youngsters. She was so poised that she could have been on a catwalk, all her movement generated from her supple, youthful hips. Tall, with beautiful dark hair and flashing eyes, she was magnetic.

I sensed a tremble of excitement in Dan as the young woman went past the barracks. She looked no more than eighteen, and clearly aware that eyes were on her, she glanced up shyly and ever so fleetingly as she passed. I heard later that she came from a much larger town than Pallas, in north County Cork, and it must have been strange for her to find herself in our village of squinting windows. We followed her every step until she passed out of sight, words between us superfluous, so precious was the moment. Dan was uncharacteristically quiet and it was by this that I judged the depth of her impact on him, as she passed on the footpath outside. I respected his silence, my own feelings, in my naivety, being an odd mixture of romance in prospect, together with already a strong sexual desire for her.

Each day thereafter, Phoebe Connell was forced to run the gauntlet of lustful eyes from any number of the gaping barrack windows. A stranger passing, and observing our wistful faces against the window panes, might be forgiven for believing the dismal building to be a place to house the deranged males of the village. And who could say but that some of us were not halfway there already, for was it not Freud who theorized that anyone possessed of a phallus unproven at twenty, risked succumbing to his violent primitive side, if not to madness itself? And though I was as yet several years short of that age, how glad I was to see her, whatever my relationship with her would prove to be.

Every afternoon thereafter Phoebe Connell went with measured stride to the post office, and grown men I had not seen smile in years were red-faced, in happy confusion, as she acknowledged them. But it was later at night when I chanced to glance through the blinds of Cunningham's pub and saw those same men, silent over their pints in the dim light, that I was reminded of some lines from that great poet Austin Clarke:

> *Men that had seen her*
> *Drank deep and were silent,*
> *The women were speaking*
> *Wherever she went —*
> *As a bell that is rung*
> *Or a wonder told shyly,*
> *And O she was the Sunday*
> *In every week.*

In a sense, however, she was treading on dangerous ground, as she strolled languidly around the place, probably not unaware of the ever-watching eyes behind flimsy curtains, some lustful, some waiting to identify a flaw, a weakness, and then to pull her down with gleeful gossip. For, given her gracious and trusting nature, she contrasted all too sharply for her own good with the few women in the village—mostly middle-aged housewives—whose timidity and fear of consequences obliged them to appear only for Sunday Mass, and furtively at that, confining themselves all week to their kitchens, and sending their men folk to the shops. And with good reason. For most groceries doubled as public houses, and a woman seen too frequently crossing the threshold of such an establishment risked being branded as a tippler or, worse, a woman of easy virtue.

Yet young Phoebe was not as fancy-free as she pretended, although she put a brave face on it. Her restlessness—she meandering each day up and down the village—intrigued and tantalized me, and may have had several explanations. But the more I watched that house for sight of her, the more I was driven to a sad conclusion. True, she was a beautiful young woman but, to my perception, she was labouring under a grave constraint, perhaps the most powerful that any young woman of her gentle and compliant disposition could have—a domineering father. When she returned from her walks to the post office, he confronted her on the lawn and seemed to interrogate her each time as to where she had been.

She promised that on each Sunday of the forthcoming festive season she would hold a party. It would be a musical evening of sorts, and she would invite young local men and girls of her own age—seventeen or eighteen—provided that each had the capacity to entertain her father. She was permitted to have as many such evenings as she liked so long as they took place on home ground, under his watchful gaze; and if those attending did not measure up, they would not be reinvited. The army had trained the colonel well.

It was on a Saturday afternoon that I received a bizarre invitation, but it was not, alas, to one of her musical evenings, for that privilege, I learnt, fell to my young tenor friend. It came, in fact, from the colonel's son, a lad called Barney, a year or two older than his sister, and, as a result, romantically speaking, the afternoon was to prove disastrous for me. Barney had many of the colonel's mannerisms. He did not laugh—he shrieked! Before he issued the invitation, I had joined him in the old church grounds where we were doing a spot of birdwatching. As he followed a blackbird in under some bushes, like a youth demented, he let out one of those deafening screams: 'Do you hear him bawling his head off in there?'

There was no answer to that. But it did enable me to reach the conclusion that his sister was the musical one.

Emerging eventually from the undergrowth, Barney suddenly looked at his watch and announced, 'I have to go. Would you like to come with us to Glenstal Abbey?'

'To the abbey? Whatever for?'

'Confession,' he answered blandly.

It was, you see, the practice of the more prominent of the villagers to avoid the embarrassment of reciting their lists of petty transgressions to the local priest and go instead to the Benedictines, many of whom, it was said, were from Belgium and had poor English and, with any luck, would take sinfulness as read, and deliver absolution swiftly, with a gentle dismissive wave.

Realizing that young Phoebe, in all possibility, would be going along, I concurred with alacrity. We drove off, the colonel at the wheel, his silent diminutive spouse by his side. With Phoebe crushed against me in the back seat and Barney seated on the other side of her, I began to wonder if it was, necessarily, the best preparation for the confessional. Far be it from me, however, to have complained.

When we arrived, Phoebe invited me to stroll with her in the woods around the old abbey grounds, but, noting the colonel's look of disapproval, I declined. She looked hurt and dismayed. I had failed her. The colonel now proposed tennis, and his wishes here had to be complied with.

As I watched Phoebe's long brown legs bounding around the court, I realized once again that only another great poet's lines could do her justice, lines from John Betjeman:

> *Love-thirty, love-forty, oh! weakness of joy,*
> *The speed of a swallow, the grace of a boy,*
> *With carefullest carelessness, gaily you won,*
> *I am weak from your loveliness, Joan Hunter Dunn.*

We drove home in darkness. Phoebe was tired beside me, her head almost resting on my shoulder, her soft lips inviting. I had, however, duly confessed at the abbey and promised a 'firm purpose of amendment'. But with her long slender thighs now hot against mine, I experienced involuntarily, and presumably therefore not sinfully, an erotic charge. In my fantasy I assumed that those half-open lips were meant for me and, turning towards her, sought them out with mine, my firm purpose of amendment swiftly crumbling.

Suddenly, I heard an unmerciful scream. It was Barney.

'Dad, there is some canoodling going on here in the back.'

His voice was bordering on the hysterical, as if his lovely sister was about to be violently impregnated. The colonel searched in his driving mirror for evidence of sinful happenings in the rear. I pulled back in alarm. Her wondrous eyes opened and met mine, with a look of utter disdain.

Confused and dismayed, I recalled having heard it said that a woman who had prepared her body to receive her male, and was at the last moment denied, would despise him ever after. As the car stopped back in the village, I felt the full force of that contempt since Phoebe climbed swiftly out and, giving me a withering look, strode away without a word, leaving me shattered.

In my youthfulness and naivety, I had been foolish to build her up as mine in my fantasy. Brought down to earth, and realizing that Dan was going to her party, I tried, with whatever grace I could muster, to abandon any claim I had harboured for her affections and to cede her, reluctantly, to him. Besides, given what he had been through, and what would be facing him in the new year, he needed her, perhaps even desperately so.

Each Sunday thereafter, in the run-up to Christmas, fresh-faced young college men foregathered at her house. Some carried musical instruments, some pathetic little parcels, others flowers. I knew that, as a mere police recruit, Dan was almost always penniless, and that he would, therefore, bring with him no petty offering but, to borrow a thought from Wilde, only his genius, for poetry, for song, for storytelling and for art itself.

When I met him after one of these soirées, he was non-committal and that was understandable. I did not pry, but I knew that it was for him a golden opportunity. For, if the romance that followed turned out to be of the whirlwind variety, the police authorities would be obliged to find him an alternative posting and that's what he desperately needed just then, to get away from the hell that Pallas had been for him with, probably, much worse to come.

The year moved swiftly to a close. The colonel did not serve alcohol and so the focus of all merriment on New Year's Eve moved decisively across to Cunningham's. It was more crowded than usual that night and, hearing singing as the midnight hour approached, I went inside where I could clearly hear Dan in full voice. His 'Ave Maria' was magnificent; next I presumed it would be 'Auld Lang Syne'. But no, he ended rather curiously, with that great war song 'Lili Marlene', his favourite air. Incredibly, I realized he was singing it in the German, which created a mood, not of celebration, but of menace, even danger. I could almost hear the tramp of goose-stepping German soldiery in the background, together with the hysterical rantings of Der Führer. It was an extraordinary rendering, doom-laden, the last repeated refrain, particularly searing: 'Wie einst Lili Marlene, Wie einst Lili Marlene'.

I wondered why he had chosen to end a night that should be one of celebration with this piece. I could only assume that, sung that way, the song reflected his mood, for given the vivid imagination I knew Dan to have, he may well have come to see the armed assignment he was to take up the following day as a kind of war. For land disputes in the area were often just that, with the police sandwiched between quarrelling factions. But in his case the situation was much worse, for the colleague who would accompany him to spend the night together in all weathers in an isolated, enclosed space was barely on speaking terms. The duration of their assignment was not specified.

But the last gesture of celebration on that New Year's Eve night belonged, as usual, to Father. A veteran of conflicts of one sort or another, he had risen on many a chilly morning at dawn to reveille, fired many a volley over a dead comrade's grave, and on sentry duty at McKee Barracks in Dublin, in his old army days, challenged many a stranger in the night. But, on New Year's Eve especially, those memories came flooding back to him.

I had often seen him at home in the evenings when the Angelus bell rang on the radio; he would suddenly jump to attention, his vast bulk sending shudders through the furniture. He would then bless himself, enjoining Mother and all seven of us in the family to do likewise, and then, doing an about-turn, army style, he would place his hat over his heart and stare out of our living-room window facing, in the distance, some imaginary symbol of Church or State or both, a flag or cross or church maybe—no one knew or dared to ask. And when on one occasion I pointed out to him that he was, in fact, facing the Protestant church, I was swiftly silenced.

But on that New Year's Eve on the stroke of midnight, there being no bells to ring in tiny impoverished Pallas, Father introduced once more his own method of ringing out the old year. He took down his rifle, whether or not legally held we feared to enquire, and going out by the moonlight to the dreary enclosed prison-like yard, my younger brother and I standing on either side of him, he levelled his rifle over the chestnut trees outside the gate, and the village beyond, and beyond that the Slieve Phelim hills.

As the volley of shots rang out, most of the villagers would probably have been preparing for bed and have reacted with some alarm, blessing themselves quickly. But then realization would dawn, 'It's only the Sergeant', whom they would then remember always went slightly barmy after a few whiskies on New Year's Eve.

But, as I crossed that gloomy yard, mere minutes into the New Year, the day my friend Dan and his resentful colleague James Byrne were to begin armed night duty as a result of the land row, the smell of cordite lingered. Ominously!

CHAPTER 11

The land dispute that was now about to occupy Dan and James Byrne in armed night protection duty reached a peak at the height of the Emergency, in the early 1940s. The headquarters of the Local Defence Force at the time was in the barracks at Pallas and, though there was little or no crime, Father had his hands full helping to direct the defence effort, the great fear at the time being of a German invasion on the south-west coast. Father was preoccupied, not only with this work, but also with helping local unemployed men join the army or the Garda Síochána, while many others sought his assistance to emigrate to Britain, or even farther afield. There were some, however, who merely wanted him to recommend them to contacts he had in Dublin, for a job in a pub there. Strong men of good farming background were always in great demand for this work, and many of these prospered.

One strapping young fellow, who sought Father's assistance to work overseas, played so vigorously for the local hurling team that the famous Mackey hurling men gave him a wide berth when he thundered down the field of play. Father, admiring his fearlessness, duly recommended him for the police service in Palestine or Hong Kong, or some such far-flung trouble spot where, in the fullness of time, he rose to high rank.

My father also took an interest in many a penniless war veteran, especially those badly injured in France and left without the merest pension for their efforts. One such pint-sized man, his body riddled with shrapnel, pumped the water for Father each day into the large tanks on the roof of the barracks. You could see his pained expression as he toiled at the pump, stopping every so often to puff on a Woodbine, the only pleasure life offered him. Unable to read or write adequately, he had failed to claim a pension. Father wrote on his behalf to His Majesty's War Office, only to be posed by way of a reply the extraordinary question, 'Was this man ever involved in violence of any sort?' Father enjoyed writing letters for those down on their luck, but none gave him greater satisfaction than his answer to that question: 'He was severely wounded fighting for your army at the Battle of the Somme. Was there ever anything more violent than that?'

The damaged little man from the Somme could soon afford a few more Woodbines and the occasional pint of porter.

Father had, however, the rather less pleasant task, during the Emergency, of monitoring those men with strongly anti-British and hence pro-German sympathies. Though some were his friends, if he deemed them a threat to the state, he was obliged to recommend them for internment in any of a number of detention centres, the main one being the Curragh Camp in County Kildare. These were, however, difficult judgments to make.

So Father had more than enough to do, along with his colleagues in the barracks, without having to keep a weather eye out for a volatile and angry young land agitator, one Timmy Cronin, from Kilduff, about half a mile from the village. And, ironically, it was this man who would cause more fear and apprehension in the area than all the armies that, at some stage or other, had threatened to invade us, but never did. These included the Germans and the British and American forces, massed across Northern Ireland, who were expected to push southwards at some point.

Though Cronin's campaign of intimidation against the Kennedys coincided with the Emergency, his father had died many years before in the world-wide flu epidemic of 1918. He left a widow and five children, the eldest and youngest both boys, with three girls in between. Timmy was the youngest, a mere child then, and his grief-stricken mother was unable to handle her new situation and developed a drink problem, which meant that she never quite made it to the rent office in the city each week. As a result, the rent fell badly in arrears. Inevitably, the children suffered neglect, the cows had to be sold and, eventually, when a solicitor's letter arrived threatening Mrs Cronin with eviction, the little holding had to be put up for sale. Alas, when a valuation was done, it was discovered that, owing to the extremely depressed national economy at the time, the place was worth no more than the outstanding rent bill.

The horse-breeding folk in the adjoining farm, the Kennedys, were sympathetic and helped the family generously with food supplies and fuel. This prompted the children's paternal grandfather, who still lived on the farm, to approach the Kennedys, along with the eldest Cronin son, Tommy, and invite them to buy some land. The Kennedys responded generously, by not only buying the entire holding, thus enabling the Cronins to pay off the rent in full, but they handed back to the stricken family the dwelling house, together with a herd of cows and enough land to keep the wolf from the Cronin door from then on. But, young Timmy, when the new legal title was drawn up, had been overlooked. On reaching adulthood, he discovered this and began a campaign of intimidation against the Kennedys, choosing to ignore the fact that they had acted very fairly and had helped feed him for a time, as a child, after his father had died and his mother had been forced to sell everything to finance her sad weakness.

As he grew to manhood, Timmy had fastened on to a few outdated ideas about land-grabbing which he understood to be the purchase by rich men of land from which poor folk had been forced out. Thereafter, wild horses could not convince him that it was a fair settlement. And here he was now in the mid-1940s threatening merry hell on the Kennedys, his family's one-time benefactors. His mother had since died and his brother Tommy had married but had no family. The three girls, now grown up, had gone to work elsewhere, but visited occasionally, as did Timmy, who was allowed to live in the family home when he began his campaign of intimidation against the Kennedys.

Father knew that Timmy had friends in the IRA and must have been tempted to recommend him for internment, if only to get him out of the way until the war was over. But he had known the fellow ever since his father had died and he probably felt an obligation to try to keep him out of trouble. Remembering his own youth, when his mother had told him that he was too fiery for policing, he had joined the defence forces and admitted that this experience had tamed him. His mother had seen him, at fifteen years of age, throwing off his jacket to fight the soldiers on seeing them smash up some of his ailing father's finest pottery pieces when they came looking for his older brother who was on the run. However, his efforts to persuade Cronin to join up were not at first as fruitful as he had hoped, but eventually Timmy did become involved in the defence effort and for most of the Emergency this ensured that he was preoccupied with something other than the land question.

Meantime, Father and his colleagues got on with the business of facilitating the Defence Forces as they prepared for the expected German invasion. To my memory, there was always an air of unreality about these preparations. True, many hundreds of local men and some women rallied to the cause and were duly kitted out in uniforms, the colour of which differentiated those who would be active, militarily speaking, from those who would be engaged in intelligence, night-patrolling, and ensuring supplies of food, fuel and other essentials for the local population.

Inevitably, there was a certain amount of cynical comment, some claiming that many farmers' sons had joined up, not to fight, but to secure the free boots and leggings that would prove useful for trudging through muddy fields and farmyards. Leather was scarce at that time and I had a grim experience myself, at age twelve or thirteen, when my regular boots needed repair, so Father equipped me with a pair of army boots for school. Many of my fellow pupils from the poorer areas were in their bare feet and paid little attention to the size of the footwear I was tramping about in. But it was the master's reaction that dismayed me for, whenever our class stood in a circle around him and he looked in my direction, his eyes travelled down to my boots and he found it difficult not to laugh. I felt humiliated, the toes of my huge army boots assuming gargantuan dimensions. I attributed my fear of being looked at, from which I suffered for years afterwards, to that master's jeering.

Gradually, however, there was disillusionment in Pallas with the war effort, especially when, after huge trenches were dug inside the hedges on the road to the city, it was discovered that the regular army was short of rifles and therefore the local force would have to face the Germans with nothing more lethal than

spades and shovels. Moreover, members of the force in the
neighbourhood were obliged to get about on bicycles, given the
shortage of petrol, and this, together with the unavailability of
rifles, brought their morale to a very low point indeed.

However, someone in their ranks came up with the bright idea
of halting the German advance a mile before they reached the
village, by partly sawing through some giant oak trees beside a
very narrow part of the Limerick road, at Wheeler's bend. The
idea was to fell the oaks at the last minute, as the advancing army
approached, in the belief that the enemy tanks would then head
off in some other direction. All this must have looked to some
of the old timers in the area, who had served in the Great War,
as game-playing bordering on the absurd. To try to reassure the
villagers, Father resolved that some show of force was necessary.
There was in his office a solitary .22 rifle that Byrne and other
officers occasionally used for shooting trout in the river; it was
useful for little else. Moreover, he had been issued with one single
army officer's uniform, to be worn by whichever garda he would
nominate to liaise with the local defence officers. He duly presented
this uniform to Stan Hollis, the most sartorially aware member in
the barracks. A fine build of a man, Hollis was immensely pleased
at the picture he presented around the village, which made it easy
for Father to then instruct him to take the .22 and stand sentry
on the roof of the barracks, looking out for the Luftwaffe, whose
arrival, Father told him, would be a sure sign that the German
invasion on the south-west coast had begun. The villagers were
quick to see the comic side of this decision, which may well have
been what Father intended, and Hollis became a laughing stock.

And so, as the threat of invasion abated, low morale among
the volunteers in Pallas gradually gave way to amusement at the

paucity of the village's defences in the event of attack, and not even Father escaped jokes being told around the village at his expense. One such referred to his good fortune at Christmas-time when, given the food shortages, others were not so lucky in sourcing traditional, seasonal food items. Father, however, was able to secure one particular item in abundance, for always in darkness very late on Christmas Eve, at least one young farmer's son would be despatched by his father or mother from somewhere beyond the Hill of Grean, with a bulky sack tied firmly to the handlebars of his bicycle. He would have been instructed to deliver the sack and contents to Father in person, and to no one else. Not being familiar with the barracks layout, he would knock loudly on the door of the barracks proper instead of coming to our quarters.

When the orderly opened the door, the lad would be seen to be grimly holding a sack, inside of which there would be a violent movement. He would then enquire, 'Is the sergeant around at all?' Whereupon, from the sack would come an eloquent explanation for this very late visitation—'Honk, Honk, Honk'. Yet another goose would then be handed over for Father. And, for years after, anyone enquiring about Father's whereabouts, to the amusement of those listening, would use that exact form of enquiry—'Is the sergeant around at all—Honk, Honk, Honk?'

And so the stage was reached when not even the gibes of the American-born, Galway-raised William Joyce, better known as Lord Haw Haw, the German propaganda broadcaster, were found other than amusing when one Sunday evening on radio he declared that 'the Irish army could not drive the tinkers out of Rathkeale'. Serious discussion of the war in the pubs at night was now giving way to hilarity at some of the reports coming in from the night patrols. A blackout of sorts was in force and the patrols went about in near darkness. One of these single patrols, a local school principal, John Bowman, perhaps the most sober man in the area, solemnly reported one morning that, at a point just beyond Wheeler's bend, he had seen something that had frozen him to the spot. Sitting on a hedge, he reported, was a most attractive young woman in floods of tears, combing her long blonde hair. When, eventually, he found enough confidence to pass her by, and looked around again, she was gone. Later, as he described the lass more fully, some folk living nearby all but swore that he was referring to a local girl whom, some years before, her jealous husband had done to death. Inevitably, given the pathetic state of the village's defences, someone suggested one night in Cunningham's pub, to uproarious laughter, that the blonde lady on the hedge, if only she had hung around long enough, and given how she had rooted the schoolmaster so effectively, might well have proven a more effective counter to the advancing enemy, had they shown up, than the rest of Pallas's defences put together.

Reports of ghostly apparitions tended to flourish during the Emergency attributable, perhaps, to the strict imposition of the nightly blackout. Father, however, was a sceptic. He claimed that he always investigated such events when he encountered them and usually found them to have a rational explanation. Once, passing an old graveyard late at night, somewhere at the back of the Hill of Grean, he saw a human skull just inside the gate, with a pair of extremely alert eyes, looking very much alive, staring out at him. Probably fortified by a whiskey or two, he dismounted from his bike and went to investigate, as a good policeman should, taking with him his chief investigative weapon, his bicycle lamp. Yet again Father insisted that he was vindicated for, as he approached, a huge wild cat leapt from inside the skull and scampered away through the tombstones.

On another late night occasion, along a bleak new road, bereft of trees or hedges, Father once heard footsteps following him, as he cycled along, buffeted by high winds and driving rain. Again he dismounted and, as soon as he did, the footsteps stopped. But, when he walked on beside his bicycle, they resumed their pursuit of him. Undaunted, he played a game of stop and start with his pursuer for a time, but could not shake him off. Yet again, notwithstanding the grim weather conditions, he felt the policeman's obligation to investigate and so he placed his bicycle against a fence and, wrenching his flashlamp from it, sought out his mysterious stalker. And, sure enough, when he shone the lamp across the fence, standing looking at him, drenched, lonely and utterly without shelter from the elements, was a poor donkey. The owner soon heard from Father and, eventually, animal welfare having become such a priority with him, for his efforts on the donkey's behalf Father received a walking stick, suitably inscribed, from the Irish Society for the Prevention of Cruelty to Animals.

Father tended, tongue-in-cheek, to claim that he had answers to most local problems, natural or supernatural. However, the answer to one strange phenomenon during the blackout seemed to elude him, yet he insisted that he would not have rested until he had solved it, but for the context being a funeral. An old member of the landed gentry class, who lived in a magnificent old house by the Mulcair river, passed away and was being waked in traditional fashion with all the neighbours and servants attending. It was a late autumn afternoon and mourners in the main front drawing room, though believing that all relatives had arrived, were surprised to see a large white automobile sweeping through the great gates several hundred yards away. Then, in the gathering gloom, they saw it move, as a shadow might when the clouds eclipse the sun, swiftly and silently through the trees that lined the long winding avenue until finally, still without making a sound on the gravel fronting the building, it disappeared around to the rear of the house.

Father was standing near the large drawing room window and was alarmed to notice something about the vehicle that startled him. Not only was there a certain shimmering unreality about the way it moved, almost as if floating on air but, as far as he could judge in the failing light, it appeared to have no occupants, not even a figure, spectral or otherwise, at the steering wheel. Father excused himself and, going swiftly to the rear of the house, found that the deceased man's widow had got there before him, only for them both to discover that there was no automobile, white or otherwise. Putting a finger over her lips to warn him not to utter a word about what they had seen to anybody, the old lady told him that it was a phenomenon that had dogged the family for years and they had come to refer to it as the 'phantom car'. Father, whenever he told that story afterwards, would speculate at length on all the possible explanations, but never very convincingly.

But now, with the war over and the blackout lifted, the blonde woman on the hedge at Wheeler's bend had gone and the speculation and laughter about her in the pubs had vanished with her, and we were all the poorer for her passing. In the village at night there was no longer the sound of tramping feet, and Hollis and his .22 rifle had, long since, come down off the barrack roof, while, on the farms and bogs, the free boots and leggings were being put to excellent use. And there was important news for me, as I went in search of state employment. A letter had come from army headquarters which said, to my astonishment and great joy, that I had given two years' local defence service and that my performance had been 'exemplary'. I wondered for a long time after if, somehow, Father had contrived to influence the wording of that letter.

There was bad news too. The phoney war was now over, but the real war, as far as Pallas was concerned, was about to begin. For, released from service in the defence forces, Timmy Cronin was back on his own private warpath. And back with a vengeance!

CHAPTER 12

'A man', playwright J. B. Keane once wrote, 'will cheerfully kill for his field' and local men who had come through the land wars of the 1880s had seen that happen many times before and did not have to be reminded that it could happen again. They knew, moreover, that before any such land feuds could be resolved, usually blood would have to be shed. That was the lesson of history. And Timmy Cronin, they believed, if he experienced again some of the wild phases he had gone through as a teenager, was well capable of exacting from Dick Kennedy that ultimate price. For Timmy never doubted that the Kennedys had taken advantage of his mother's plight, after his father's sudden death, and had acquired, for little or nothing, those precious fields that Timmy now wanted them to give back, or face grievous consequences.

But, in view of the fact that he had been left fatherless so young and his mother's mental health had all but disintegrated after that, it was inevitable that Timmy would have problems. Whoever influenced him thereafter, his paternal grandfather apart, did him no favours, given how poorly he understood what had happened to the family after his father's death.

The Kennedys were understandably dismayed when the fellow whom, as a child, they had helped to feed, had now begun to harass them at every opportunity. But Timmy, then in his thirties, was a very angry young man, with a mentality not mediated by humour or proportion and, if anything, more volatile and unpredictable than his mother. What surprised Father, however, was that despite his fierce temper, Timmy had actually avoided getting into trouble when in the army, which left him wondering if there was not a element of bluff in his campaign of intimidation against the Kennedys.

Timmy's first statement of intent was contained in an anonymous letter he fired off to the Kennedys, advising them to take the precaution of placing an order for their burial coffins with the local undertaker, a not unusual form of threat in the old land war days of the 1880s. The Kennedys went forthwith to the garda barracks, requesting police protection. This was quickly approved and two experienced detectives deployed, temporarily, until Dan Duff was ready to accompany his thirty-nine-year-old colleague, James Byrne, on this special duty. Alas, the two had nothing in common except for being members of the same force and being the only two at the station qualified to carry arms after police headquarters had withdrawn the two detectives from Limerick.

Dan was a few months short of twenty years old when he came to Pallas and just over one year later was assigned to armed night protection duty. Because he was so young then, Father probably anticipated that his youth and inexperience might prove a handicap in coping with the often querulous Byrne and also with Timmy Cronin. Cronin was known to have access to arms, if he needed them, and the last thing Father wanted was that Dan and Cronin would confront one another some night at Mount Catherine, for both were impetuous and, given Cronin's anger with the Kennedys and Dan's determination not to fail in the responsibility entrusted to him, there was no knowing what might happen.

By the time the night duty assignment came up, Dan had gained a certain amount of experience in routine policing, but the armed assignment was a considerable step-up in responsibility. Father had probably assumed that Dan's stint in the army, in which he had done well, had matured him beyond his years. The circus incident, even if distressing, had been a valuable experience, and he had more than once been given assignments to recover stolen goods, and had carried them out successfully.

On one occasion, when a wheel had been stolen from the back of a truck in the village, Father sent Dan to the household where he suspected the wheel had probably been hidden. He told Dan to make a friendly call to the house in question and tell the family that he, the sergeant, wanted their assistance in recovering the wheel. Dan's diplomatic skills proved effective and the wheel was handed in to the barracks the next day, with the explanation that 'one of the lads' had found it behind a hedge on the road to Nicker.

On another occasion, Dan and Father were together when a visitor collided with a local man's car near the village. Father quickly discovered that the visitor was a friend of his from a former posting in the midlands and was clearly at fault in the crash. He knew, however, that the local man did not have insurance for his vehicle, so both drivers were at fault in their different ways. A more orthodox officer would simply have prosecuted the two men, one for dangerous driving, the other for failing to insure his vehicle, but that was not Father's way. Instead, he took out his measuring tape and sent Dan and the local man down the road as far as the tape would stretch, to measure the skid-marks, visible or not, made by the visitor's car.

While they were gone, he took his visiting friend aside and said to him, 'Look. Ask the driver when he returns if he has insurance.'

The visitor duly posed the question, while Father moved out of earshot and the next time he turned around the two men were shaking hands. Father, as he got older, had discovered that if in the course of his duties he could win friends and influence people, he should do so. Dale Carnegie would have been proud of him. And so all went together to Cunningham's snug and, as Dan told me later, the collision was never mentioned again.

On another occasion Father and Dan joined forces to challenge a local farmer about unlicensed dogs. On their arrival at the farm, they found the mud so deep that they were soon embedded and had to communicate with the fellow from more than fifty paces away. Cows, pigs and greyhounds were seemingly everywhere. The hounds were chasing around the farmhouse at great speed, the farmer encouraging them as they went. Father asked the fellow how many he had. 'Half a dozen or so', he answered. 'Ah, come on, Billy,' Father shouted back at him. 'You must have as many as twelve or fifteen hounds chasing around there, by my count.' 'Arragh, not at all, Sergeant', he roared; 'they're the same feckin' dogs you're countin', comin' round again.' Father looked at Dan in dismay, admitting defeat, something he did not like having to do, but it could not but have helped the rookie to see there were times when a police officer had to back off and rethink a problem, and try to find a solution later.

Because Father would never discuss Dan with me, I always assumed that he had full confidence in his capacity to handle the night duty assignment, given his army background. Besides, I knew it was part of Dan's make-up to embrace any challenge, for his belief in himself, especially when first he came to Pallas, seemed to me to be total.

However, the Kennedys, whom he and Byrne would be

protecting, soon made a crucial misjudgment: they socialized with
the superintendent and his wife, both couples childless and both
wives said to be unhappy with their lot. And, very likely influenced
by the superintendent, the Kennedys decided that they did not
propose to offer the merest facility, not even a cup of tea or a
place to shelter, to the two men who would spend all night in all
weathers ensuring that the couple slept safely in their beds. I had
the impression that Father feared that this casual indifference to the
welfare of his men by the very people they were protecting could
have serious consequences for their morale.

But the Kennedys were always a little out of touch with the
lives of the ordinary people, though it was thought around the
village that they had a blessed existence and that if you had land
and property, not to mention good looks, fashion and horses,
then you had it all. However, the fact was that the Kennedys,
like everyone else, had their problems and these were now vastly
compounded by Timmy Cronin's campaign of intimidation,
about to resume with a far greater intensity. So there was genuine
sympathy around the area for them, despite their maintaining a
rather aloof stance from the local people.

Ellen Kennedy's sole interest was fashion and many wondered if
she ever fully fitted in at Mount Catherine. Moreover, it was well
known that those from that robust male preserve, the racing and
bloodstock world, which was Dick Kennedy's preserve, were more
likely, whether with horses or women, to focus rather less on the
actual harness worn and more on the body beneath, its classiness
or lack of it, and of course its breeding potential. But those few
who knew the Kennedys best held the view that, ironically, ever
since Timmy Cronin had first voiced his anger at them, it had
served only to drive the childless couple closer together.

However, the stage was now set for a showdown in this long-running land agitation, centred on Mount Catherine. The two men from the barracks would be hanging around all night in the cold and wet, feeling isolated and vulnerable. Holed up with his wife in his mansion would be Dick Kennedy, a shotgun not far away, while lurking somewhere in the long grass Timmy Cronin was awaiting his opportunity.

Father was familiar with the layout of Mount Catherine and the Kilduff area generally, for he visited the Kennedys and the Cronins many times in those early days of the dispute, endeavouring to broker a compromise which, alas, was never even a remote prospect. On one extraordinary occasion the Kennedys actually called Father to the farm when, apparently, there had been a break-in and Ellen's valuable box of jewellery had gone missing. The first thing he noted when he looked around was that the interior of the house seemed to be in perfect order and that would be an odd thing if there had been a burglary. Knowing something of the stress the Kennedys were under, he soon concluded that one of the pair was playing tricks on the other. The problem was which one. To give himself time to think, he looked around the house and concluded from her demeanour that Ellen was probably the guilty one. The problem was first to find the missing jewellery box. His policeman's gut instinct told him that it was probably hidden outside the house, and sure enough, under a newspaper, in the back seat of a vintage Rolls parked forlornly by the side of the house, was the missing box. He decided not to make things worse by confronting them. So, handing her valuable collection back to Ellen, he said casually, 'Ye were lucky. The blackguard was about to drive off with it when ye arrived back and disturbed him.'

Whereupon the couple embraced warmly and Father went on his way, wondering if had not missed out on his true vocation: solving family rows instead of crime.

But it was a disappointment now to him that the Kennedys, whom he had helped out time and again, did not propose to be more humane in looking after his two men when they began this protection duty in the Kennedy backyard. I saw him fume with anger when the superintendent told him. He most probably knew that Duff and Byrne were not exactly bosom pals, but he hoped that they would bury their differences, having been thrown together through necessity. But it must have worried him more than he admitted, given that all three parties were armed, to know that the two protectors in the land issue were almost as much at odds with one another as the respective disputants.

The villagers probably viewed the conflict with even more foreboding than Father, for they knew more than anyone the depth of resentment that land rows generated and they would have expected it to be a war of attrition in and around Mount Catherine, and probably a question of who cracked first.

By this time Father was resigned. There was nothing else he could do, since his hands had been tied by the intransigence of police headquarters who insisted that he deal with the land row out of the pool of officers at his disposal. Moreover, his relationship with the superintendent was not the best, the men not seeing eye to eye on several issues.

Father was also beginning to show his age, and his capacity to delegate responsibilities to others had never been his strong point. Sometimes I saw him in those days as a King Lear-like figure, his former powers on the wane, and the increased poundage around his girth becoming more and more evident. He went more frequently to

Kilteely, a little village at the back of the Hill of Grean, where fellow south-coast folk ran a pub and a post office. I came to believe they were the only true confidants he had. But he had a Houdini-like record of survival already and, whatever happened, we all believed that the native cunning of the Corkonian in him would see him through. He had a constant battle of wills with the postmistress at Pallas. He was deemed to be the font of all knowledge in the area, but he knew that she was the omniscient one, for all phone calls passed through her exchange and it was believed that she listened in to everything. Yet it was the volume of letters that she steamed open which bothered Father most. Some of these anonymous poison-pen missives accused him and his men of neglecting to deal with after-hours drinking in the pubs, and outlined the gambling, drinking and flagrant womanizing of some of his officers. As a consequence, he could never take holidays, for he could not allow these letters to get into the hands of the superintendent, to whom many of them would have been addressed. So he went personally to the post office every morning and, collecting the bundle of mail, turned over every single item on its back, under the gaze of the postmistress herself, to show her that he knew that she was steaming them open. She never batted an eyelid. On his return to the station, he selected first the most vitriolic ones and, making a little fire in his grate, got rid of them—before they got rid of him.

In earlier postings he had to deal with difficult situations created by visitors to the respective towns. The first was none other than Countess Markievicz, who arrived for an election rally in Edenderry, County Offaly in June 1927 and drove around the place like a mad thing, ignoring all traffic laws, for she detested the governing party, including its uniformed representatives, with all her heart. Given that the townspeople were looking on with

a critical eye at their much-vaunted, new police force, Father
had no option but to confront her. It must have been with some
trepidation that he did so, if he knew then that, with evident pride
in her achievement, she was supposed to have shot a policeman in
the back of the head during the 1916 affair. When Father faced
the Countess, she towered over him, dressed in some outlandish
garb, and he told her that if she could not produce papers for her
vehicle, he had powers to arrest her. 'You wouldn't dare, Sergeant,'
she exploded. He informed her that he would not hesitate.
However, some accommodation was reached, but soon afterwards
Father found himself removed to a hovel of a station with no
running water in Cleggan, County Galway. Mother, carrying
her first child, languished in exile until he fought his way out of
Connemara by writing letters to former colleagues who had risen
in the ranks. While there, he spent his time searching for stolen
sheep and illicit poteen among the hostile islanders of Inishbofin
who, unlike him, spoke only in the native tongue. He wondered
ever afterwards if that awful posting had to do with his encounter
with the brave Countess, for the party she supported assumed
power soon after their contretemps.

However, ill luck struck Father again, after he had fought
his way back to the midlands, to Abbeyleix, County Laois, an
excellent town that Mother loved and, unlike Pallas later, it had
good shopping, boys' and girls' secondary schools and better
prospects of job opportunities for her growing brood. But when
a troupe of dancing girls in short skirts hit town in February 1931
and danced in the much-revered town hall, the Catholic clergy
and the Legion of Mary joined forces in implacable opposition
and, in writing, requested everyone to support the protest. The
letter in question was headed 'Catholic Action Committee' and

was signed by no fewer than nineteen businessmen in the town, plus two clergymen. Yet though the letter was the outcome of a special meeting to discuss the indecency of the length of the young dancing girls' skirts, not a single female from the town was invited to take part in the discussion. The letter read as follows:

A Chara,

The above committee earnestly request your attendance outside the Town Hall, Abbeyleix, on to-night (Saturday) at 8 p.m., and tomorrow (Sunday) night at the same hour, to support their protest against the unseemly entertainment which is at present being carried on in the Hall.

No Catholic should fail in his duty regarding this matter.

In the event, the members of the quite large Protestant community did not regard the semi-naked thighs of the dancing girls as being in the least bit offensive and, inevitably, Father was called in to determine the rights and wrongs of the situation. He had no doubt but that the law was firmly on the side of the dancing girls and, together with garda reinforcements from nearby, he duly cleared a passage each night to allow anyone wishing to attend the performance to do so in peace. But he paid a price! He was approached by an irate member of the clergy who said to him, 'Sergeant, you need not have interfered; we could have kept the peace of the town ourselves.' Father's reply was uncompromising. 'That, Father, is my job, not yours.' Within months, a notification of a transfer to Pallas was on his desk, with no reason given. It took a great deal of letter-writing before he was told why he was being transferred to Pallas. The answer revealed the dreadful state of the relationship between the Garda Síochána and the Roman Catholic clergy at the time. The letter from the Secretary of the

Representative Body of the Garda Síochána, signed illegibly in Irish, read as follows:

Dear Sergeant,

Just a note to say the question of your transfer was brought under my notice during the recent provincial Representative Body meeting, and I have enquired into the matter—to be quite candid I asked the Commissioner today about it. The root of the trouble is that you are having some difficulty with the R.C. Clergy and in that difficulty not one of your authorities has even suggested that you have acted any way but manly and honourably. As a matter of fact, the Commissioner has made this plain in ordering your transfer and directed that you get the best station available.

Of course the matter could be pressed but would the position be any happier for you now? Bad feeling would arise between Clergy and Gardaí generally here and it would be hard to say where it would end. I know you were wrongly treated but you must remember that this is a very, very Catholic country—I would not say Christian country, and Clergy are at the moment all powerful and very bitter enemies, and if we had left you there they would have made your life a hell. You are being sent to Pallas which is regarded as a very good station. You can be sure that your record is unblemished.

You can drop me a note and let me have your views. I am only too happy to do everything possible where a man is not getting a fair deal.

Best wishes.

Sincerely yours,

SECRETARY

And so by the time he came to be involved in Timmy Cronin's campaign in Pallas, Father had learnt a few lessons, and one of these was perhaps that it was better not to rush with undue haste into other people's rows. This could have been one of the reasons why he was absent from Nicker Church on that unforgettable Sunday morning when everyone knew that Cronin was going to make a stand.

CHAPTER 13

Cronin's anonymous letter to the Kennedys was a grave misjudgment, for it was so threatening that they could hardly believe that a sane man would have penned it, and it served only to make them determined not to communicate with him, but to apply immediately for Garda protection. Cronin had made the mistake of using the tactics of another era, when the land wars of the 1880s had torn the country apart and intimidation of this sort was commonplace. And so his action had ensured that if there had been a chance of his reaching some accommodation with the Kennedys before then, now there was none.

Some people learn from their mistakes, but Cronin was not one of those and, instead of pulling back from his threat that dire things would now befall the Kennedys, he set about intensifying his campaign. Rumour swept the village that on a forthcoming Sunday there would be violent scenes after eleven o'clock Mass. The villagers, especially the more God-fearing of the womenfolk, were dismayed at such an unholy prospect at Nicker Church, of all places. What, they asked, was the world coming to?

Timmy knew that this Mass was not only by far the best attended one, but also the top social event of the week, when most of the local population foregathered in their Sunday best, ostensibly to serve the Lord but, if the truth were faced, even more to be part of the social whirl. It was outside Nicker Church that, in general and local elections, politicians of every hue stood on the backs of trucks and harangued the 'faithful' with the tired old rhetoric we had heard a hundred times before.

Timmy Cronin, however, was not looking for votes or money, but simply for support from his neighbours to implement a boycott against the Kennedys, which would mean that they would be shunned in the streets and the shops until they acknowledged the error of their ways. And, having done so, he hoped that then they would have the good sense to cede to him the land that, as he saw it, they had so cunningly misappropriated when values were so low that it bordered on the criminal to pay only the rock-bottom price for it. Cronin took the view that land was far more than merely a patch of ground; it was a means of making a living, and the price at which it had changed hands, twenty-five years before, should, he thought, have reflected that fact.

But the locals believed that Cronin was living in the past. Back in the nineteenth century, common sense had held sway in regard to the value of land, but now the notion of 'the market price' was beginning to rule and the people of Pallas were not impressed by Cronin's outdated logic. Moreover, the farming folk around Pallas had become more secure and more comfortably off and, therefore, had grown complacent. There had been a time in Ireland when the land question was so emotive that people rallied to the cause of any man who felt hard done by. But no longer.

Besides, Cronin was no orator and most unlikely to sway to his flag any more than a handful of like-minded malcontents. The fear was, however, that like many a hot-headed country boy before him, he could well resort to violence, if words of abuse failed him. And that was why on that particular Sunday, as local folk made their way to eleven o'clock Mass, there was an expectation of high drama.

The church in question, in the tiny village of Nicker, nestles at the foot of the Hill of Grean, its grotto a natural cave-like space driven in under the hill. In earlier times, Mass was celebrated furtively on the summit, facilitated by a deep hollow, around which the weather-beaten peasantry knelt in devotion to the sacrament. Meanwhile, lookout men at various vantage-points peered across the valley for signs of Crown forces in pursuit of the fugitive celebrant who, if caught, would at best be imprisoned, but sometimes summarily executed. And so, in those difficult times, it was not only in the context of land agitation, but of worship too, that the uniformed representatives of the governing power were feared and distrusted, not just in our part in Limerick, but countrywide.

The church itself, of Romanesque design, is laid out with a nave and four side aisles. An outlay of sixpence was obligatory to gain entrance to the nave, the preferred term being an 'offering'. And, though not strictly speaking an admission charge, brave would be the man or woman who would pass the stern-faced official with outstretched plate without depositing thereon a coin at the very least of silver complexion. The presentation of one or two of copper variety would be deeply frowned upon.

Entrance to the side aisles required an offering of threepence, while the two aisles way out on the wings could be entered for as little as a penny. These wing aisles, as the scale of the offering indicated, were draughty places where each Sunday the labouring folk of the area languished and, being unencumbered by property or money, or, for that matter, airs and graces, a greater devotion by them to the sacred happenings on the altar was always discernible, though their view of the altar, ironically, was partially obscured. But no Pharisees were they, being largely indifferent to the sartorial distractions for which the nave was noted and so, heads down in their humility, they beat their breasts more assiduously than the rest of us.

The side aisles were occupied mainly by farming men and women in heavy serge suits, with ruddy countenances and large, calloused hands. And, in truth, it was they who were the only true workhorses present, putting as they did, unacknowledged, bread and butter on the table for the rest of us. However, throughout the proceedings their concentration was probably less on the altar and more on concerns back at the farm, invariably to do with sick animals, fearful weather forecasts and plummeting prices for their hard-won produce.

But it was the nave that was the veritable fashion walk, at the top of which the self-selected elite of Pallas assembled in their finery. The rest of us in that august segment, mostly with white collar pretensions, languished in the rear, much less assured that we deserved our place in the sun. However, it was the seeming certainty of the *crème de la crème* farther up the nave that they had already earned salvation that was mind-blowing, as they sat, the picture of self-satisfaction, many using their very own pews, adorned with their names in gold plate, to minister unto their vanity. And in the topmost pew, as near as made no difference to the altar of God, sat Dick and Ellen Kennedy.

Behind the Kennedys, also in that exclusive upper half of the nave, were a group of leading lights of the shop-keeping and pub-owning community. Along with these were a handful of senior members of the teaching profession and then, alas, two cuckoos in that exclusive nest. One of these was the sartorially impeccable womanizer from the barracks, Stan Hollis, while a pew behind him, Pioneer pin in place in his lapel, sat the enigma of the barracks, the furtive mystery man who, as his preferred recreation, accompanied handsome fourteen-year-old youths to the cinema at Cappamore, County Limerick, a safe four miles away. For it seemed it was only in the dark interior of such a place that James McCabe could relax with his passive, unsuspecting companions.

As my brother Jamie and I hurried uphill to the church on that particular Sunday, the faces of those around us, especially the older women, reflected the widespread apprehension that there would be angry scenes after Mass. Inevitably, some of the younger men, who often witnessed violent clashes on the hurling field on Sundays, or bouts of fisticuffs on fair days, were not perturbed, possibly even welcoming a little after-Mass blood-letting, to provide a talking point for the afternoon.

I felt a knot of anxiety grip my stomach as we got nearer the church, for I was reminded of that unpleasant night of the circus and was fearful that there would again be bloody conflict. As we passed the old national school, memories of fierce fistfights at lunchtime came flooding back, heightening my apprehension. I recalled how the school bully, Dundon, used to invite all and sundry out to fight; my older brother, Mike, once took him on, the two of them rolling on the ground and punching hell out of one another. And, since the fight was taking place on the road, outside the school grounds, which was not the Master's area of responsibility, he looked on approvingly, one leg up on the wall, as he peeled his daily apple after lunch. A boxing fan, there was fire in the Master's eyes as he all but egged on the combatants and then, pocketing his penknife, clapped his hands loudly, commanding us all to return to class, as Mike and Dundon, with bloodied noses, picked themselves up from the dust.

But these memories of times past faded swiftly as Jamie and I entered Nicker Church, which was all but full, hushed and expectant. There were a few latecomers, as a handful of self-consciously upper-crust folk from the community paraded up the nave, their arrival timed to perfection. Then, suddenly, a bell rang angrily—all too angrily, intensifying my pent-up anxiety. The celebrant, chalice held aloft, emerged from behind the altar, followed by four vulnerable-looking boys, suitably attired. Mass got underway.

As Jamie and I squeezed into a rear seat of the nave, despite my nervousness and fearfulness I was keen not to miss the expected confrontation outside, when all the prayers for peace and goodwill on earth were done. Happily, Jamie seemed oblivious of the rumours of trouble to come, and all morning I had tried to conceal my apprehension.

There was as yet no sign of Timmy Cronin, but the other key players, the Kennedys, were, in a manner of speaking, on the stage. I glanced quickly behind the pay-desk in the church porch and, to my surprise, the familiar, burly figure of Father was conspicuous by its absence.

No one knew why, during Mass, Father remained in the porch, head down and on one knee. I always suspected that for him to bend two knees to any institution or cleric would be asking that bit too much, given what he had suffered at the hands of churchmen and of politicians. Some local people said that he remained in the porch to protect the accumulated cash, while others suggested darkly that it was significant that he never allowed his sons to serve on the altar.

It was notable that the men of the cloth did not take sides in the land row, because they would have been sympathetic to the plight of Timmy Cronin, for only through the possession of a few acres of land, in that dire period, could he earn a living, short of emigrating. Father probably was of the same view, though I never heard him express it.

The last gospel had scarcely concluded when not merely hurling men, but drinking men too, left the church like cattle in a stampede. In any Mass the consecration is, of course, the high point. But that morning one would be forgiven for thinking that there was another climactic event yet to come outside, and it would probably be at the very moment the Kennedys passed through those wrought-iron gates leading from sacred ground to neutral territory. In their expectation of the forthcoming excitement, many piled down the church steps in more unseemly haste than usual. The Kennedys, dignified of bearing to match their station, left last of all and, if they knew of the rumours that they would at some point come under attack, they showed no outward sign of it. Most of us knew, however, that if Cronin showed up, in all probability it would be at the last moment, for it was often said that the oddball had in his personality a greater sense of the dramatic than the rest of us. However, as we paused outside and noted how few parishioners were moving towards their cars or ponies and traps, there was no mistaking but that confrontation was in the very air.

The Kennedys took the last few steps on to the open road. They were surrounded by a few Mass-goers who, with them, represented the cream of Pallas society. Those nearest to the Kennedys appeared to be on edge. Meantime, for safety, Jamie and I remained inside the church gate. Even Jamie had now sensed that something was going to happen. And he was right, for there was a flurry, a scattering of Mass-goers just outside the gate, and then an unmerciful scream: 'Land-grabbers! Land-grabbers! Land-grabbers!' It was indeed Timmy Cronin. Jumping out from behind the large gate pillar, he danced, still shouting, in between and around the Kennedys, like a man demented. Their friends moved aside. The Kennedys were alone with Cronin. They looked shaken as the shouting continued while Timmy's hair, flying in the breeze, made him look more angry than he was normally, his expression apoplectic. As the Kennedys tried to move towards their car, with no uniformed policeman in sight, Cronin followed them. It was an extraordinary scene and looked all the more absurd, given the over-glamorous way Ellen Kennedy was dressed.

When in public, the Kennedys normally walked side by side but at least a yard and a half apart, the lady clearly wishing to render less obvious the true extent to which her husband towered over her. To help further diminish any notion that she was the lesser half, she had worn to Mass an eye-catching off-white fashion garment unbuttoned and revealing what the God-fearing locals probably considered an alarming, if not indecent, depth of cleavage. Thus she ensured that she, and not her husband, was a focus before all eyes.

But her clever tactic backfired that morning, for Timmy Cronin took full advantage and continued to dance in between the pair, making the scene look more and more like a pantomime. The Kennedys managed, finally, to close ranks as they moved towards their car, with Timmy still jigging rings around them and shouting that old refrain from the land wars, 'Land-grabbers, Land-grabbers, Land-grabbers.' He finally sent them on their way by pounding with his fist on the roof of their car. And then, as they drove off, this wild-looking thirty-year-old, probably sensing that he had received little support from his fellow-parishioners, cleared a fence and decamped across the fields. As he went, the main reaction of the now departing congregation seemed to be surprise, but also amusement and, undoubtedly, some unspoken admiration for the Kennedys' composure.

Any members of the garda present would have been in plain clothes and, almost certainly, would have reported what they had seen to Father. But the parishioners inevitably would have expressed surprise that there were no uniformed officers present who could have intervened and saved the Kennedys the humiliation of being pilloried in the presence of so many locals. But, on reflection, they would most probably have guessed that there would be consequences for Cronin, and that Father, in his unconventional fashion, would take action in own way and in his own time.

And they would not have been far wrong if they surmised that early on the next morning he would mount his bicycle and quietly depart the slumbering village of Pallas. Before doing so, he would stuff into his trouser pocket a single scrap of paper with the legend 'Summons' written thereon. He would, in due course, arrive at the Cronin household and in all likelihood Tommy, his wife and Timmy would be expecting him. And they would offer him tea and he would sit with them for half an hour and chat about the weather and the crops and the previous day's football game. But throughout he would not utter a word about the incident outside the church. And then, having finished his tea, he would rise, offer thanks for the hospitality and make to go. But when he had reached the door, as if in an afterthought, with the merest movement of his head, he would indicate to Timmy to follow him outside. He would then, all in one discreet movement, extract from his pocket his bicycle clips and along with them the piece of paper he had come to deliver. And this he would press gently into Timmy's hand with the words, 'See you Tuesday week at the courthouse at eleven o'clock. You will probably get probation. Don't be late.'

But, as he cycled away, Father would have known that the Sunday morning's events were mere preliminaries. For, in the absence of local support, unlike the old land war days, Timmy's campaign would now almost certainly go underground and what form that would take could only be guessed at. And, given that the eleventh hour had already passed, Father would have known that the consequences for Pallas could be grave indeed.

CHAPTER 14

'The man who made all men equal' was a famous remark once made about Samuel Colt, the inventor of the revolver that bore his name. And judging by my friend Dan's mood on the first night of the armed night-duty assignment, possession of a similar weapon, a Webley, did seem to boost his confidence, his sense that it put him on equal terms with just about anybody, including Timmy Cronin and James Byrne.

I watched Dan cleaning his gun before loading it that first night. Before doing so, for my entertainment, he twirled the thing several times in his right hand. Then, placing it in the right-hand pocket of his greatcoat, he went suddenly into a crouched position and drew it so fast, I hardly saw the movement. It was a little scary. He was exuding energy and restlessness as if he was about to go into combat, when in fact he was likely to find the assignment unremittingly boring, especially given the presence of Byrne, who had not a kindly word to say to him. But why, I wondered, was he in a good mood that first night? The weapon would be a protection of sorts, but would it do anything for him in the face of one of Byrne's verbal onslaughts?

On hearing Byrne tramping about upstairs, Dan suddenly adopted a more serious mood and proceeded to load the weapon. He bent over the flickering kerosene lamp and, extracting five penile-shaped little killers from his pocket, began to insert them into five of the chambers, making sure to leave the chamber under the hammer empty.

'Why?' I asked.

'It's the regulation—a precaution to prevent the gun from being fired too hastily.'

'But', I said in some alarm, 'it leaves you at a split-second disadvantage and in the meantime the other fellow may have plugged you.'

He smiled at my lack of understanding of the constraints that an armed police officer is under.

'A police officer must wait until there is a gun actually pointing at him before he may discharge his weapon.'

'Which puts you at an even greater disadvantage.'

'True, but, my friend, that goes with the job.'

He smacked the Webley shut and returned it to the right-hand pocket of his greatcoat, which he buttoned up, his smile fading, as Byrne came in.

Byrne never bothered to acknowledge people when he entered a room, except to announce his presence with a cough. With his back turned to us, he ponderously donned his greatcoat, moving his Webley from hand to hand as he did so. We watched him in silence, knowing his moodiness. He cleared his throat and, to my surprise, before buttoning up his greatcoat, stuffed his Webley, muzzle downwards, into his hip pocket. The barrack orderly, for that day, who was semi-crippled with arthritis, watched him, knowing that the manner in which Byrne had pocketed his weapon was against regulations. In disgust, the orderly spat copiously into the ailing turf fire, poking apart the three sods of turf, to find a suitably blazing part for his aim. Paradoxically, Byrne was known to be a stickler for regulations.

The two officers were soon ready to depart. Byrne led the way, knowing that Dan would follow obediently as one's dog does, so there was no need to acknowledge him. It was Byrne's way of keeping the younger man in his place. Byrne saw Dan as a probationer, a lad of no great consequence; if Dan made a fuss of this nightly humiliation, he would find himself suspended. A word in the ear of Byrne's friend, the superintendent, was all that would be required.

I watched them go out. Byrne was tall, somewhat flat-footed and slow-moving, his thin pointed face, with its narrow forehead, inscrutable. His lips were tight, like many men of immovable convictions who enjoy uniforms and uniformity, rules and regulations, and authority over others. He was rarely animated about anything. As he went, I noted the ominous bulge near his right hip and could not help wondering that if he had to get that weapon out quickly some night, he would rue the day he bypassed the regulations he professed to cherish. He cleared his throat once more, his way of informing Dan that he had better be ready to fall into step with him and be prepared to wait obediently until spoken to, the timing of which conversation, if any, Byrne, and Byrne alone, would decide.

One could see that the two men were careful to avoid anyone noticing their reciprocal coolness. Yet I knew from his expression that Dan was boiling up inside, in carefully concealed anger at this treatment of him, and wondering if there was any way out of his predicament. How long more he could endure it was hard to judge, but I knew that everyone has a breaking point.

It was, of course, possible that Byrne was feeling the strain of night duty too, though some said that he was as hard as nails. But, for better or worse, the two were now tied to one another, as if with a ball and chain, having not only to spend all night on duty together, but also to sleep in the dormitory side by side and probably dine face to face, if not in the kitchen, in a room at the back of the kitchen which was used on some occasions.

There was a strict rule that alcohol should not be taken while on duty, but in a small place like Pallas, with eight men at the station, most with little to do, it was an impossible regulation to implement rigidly, given especially that there were seven pubs in the village and many more in nearby Nicker, Old Pallas and Kilteely. Father never used alcohol when he had first come to Pallas, until one day Dr McEnery from Doon, six miles away, was driving through the village and stopped for a word with Father, who, leaning a powerful uniformed elbow through the open window of the car for a brief confab, asked him for a remedy for indigestion. 'Sergeant,' the medic advised, 'take a half-whiskey before your meal and it won't trouble you again.' Thereafter, when Father was sometimes late for dinner, Mother would say how she wished that the good doctor had stuck with the age-old remedy of bread soda.

And so for many of the gardaí in Pallas, a visit to a pub, when off duty, was customary and Dan and Byrne were no exceptions. When they rose around noon, they would have lunch and then visit separate pubs for an hour or two before taking their evening meal in the barracks at about six o' clock, though not always together. I had a sense, however, that the effects of their drinking had not always worn off by the time they were due to depart on night duty at ten o' clock and that they seemed on better terms when sober than with drink taken. Drunk or sober, however, it looked unlikely that their night duty would unite them. They were galaxies apart.

Sometimes, in the late morning, when I descended from my eyrie on the top floor of the barracks, I looked in on the two men in the dormitory to see if they wished me to run an errand for them. They were, as a rule, sitting up in bed for there were no chairs or tables. Dan was usually scribbling away in a jotter with many more full of his verse piled up at his bedside, while Byrne was poring over a law book, trying to cram his unwilling brain for the exams that would see him promoted to sergeant and transferred to another station. Little did he suspect, alas, that when, on occasion, he was seen disappearing upstairs with a large tome under his arm, some of his colleagues looked at one another, scepticism at his prospects written on their faces.

The fact that I was critical of Byrne flowed more from his hostile treatment of Dan than from any ill will I bore him. Indeed, I felt compassion for him because he seemed the loneliest man in the building and pined continually for a barrack cook in a former posting at Farranfore, County Kerry, who was apparently the only woman who had ever showed affection for him.

And so, when Byrne asked me to accompany him with the superintendent's hounds to the long lush fields down by the river, I rarely declined. His conversation on these marathon walks was usually confined to admiration for the said hounds' muscular backsides. This part of their anatomy, depending on how much it bulged, was apparently the acid test of how well he was carrying out the superintendent's instructions, which were to render the animals ready for optimum performance in one of those famous hound-coursing venues all over the south of the country.

On one of these trips, Byrne brought along his .22 rifle so that, on our return journey, we could pause at the old bridge over the Mulcair river and shoot a few trout for supper, against the regulations or not. Byrne handed me the dogs' leads as he took aim. Then bang, and several trout turned over, dead. I was despatched to a shallow part of the river farther down, to retrieve the catch, Byrne telling me, 'Go get the little bastards; you'll know them by their white bellies turned upwards.'

Though I was fearful that I might drown, Byrne's command was not something one easily disobeyed and so, wading in nervously, I grabbed the dead trout as they passed, some escaping my grasp, the slippery devils ending up downstream in the distant Shannon. Byrne, when I returned, pulled out his penknife and, repeating with glee the phrase 'the little bastards', cut off their heads and threw them to the hounds who gobbled them up, as Byrne smacked his lips in anticipation of a tasty supper to come.

It occurred to me, while the animals showed their fangs and snarled at one another jealously, that Byrne too showed his teeth only when he was killing something, whether rabbit, hare or fish. And that made me ask myself the question, as we strolled quietly the last mile home, if in a tight corner and carrying a gun, he would find it easy to kill, not merely a fish, but even a man.

That was on my mind as he and Dan went out together to Mount Catherine on that first night. I knew the road there extremely well. It would take them about twenty minutes to reach the house. Much of their walk would be in silence, if my own walks with Byrne were anything to go by, but, as Dan hinted to me later, Byrne was unpredictable. Sometimes he would lapse into silence, but at others, he would lecture Dan about the proper way to perform his night duty.

Dan's tendency, when walking after dark, was to gaze in wonder at the night sky. Byrne, on the other hand, scrutinized the road at his feet and quickly pocketed, like a child, any screws, bolts or other curiosities he found along the way. Nothing in the night sky interested him. It was yet another reflection of the awesome emotional gulf that separated these men. But then, in fairness to Byrne, Dan had not the slightest interest in the hound-coursing world and simply could not understand why Byrne devoted so many of his waking hours to little else.

On nearing Mount Catherine, they would turn sharp left and go through the great gates of the estate, past the unoccupied gate lodge and up the winding avenue between the trees. The deep gravel would crunch under their feet and it would be this sound that would announce to the Kennedys that their protectors had arrived, even though, as far as I knew, they had never met the men face to face, though that would be surprising, especially in summer months.

In the early days of the assignment, the duo tended to find that the Kennedys' master bedroom was lit up, which vexed them, for it did not make their job any easier. Ellen, in her defiant way, it was whispered locally, did not propose to alter one whit her practice, as she prepared for bed, of enjoying the wonderful sight of watching the moon lighting up the distant hills. Rumours circulated that she was sometimes rather scantily dressed, and that this may have been part of the attention-seeking behaviour that she tended to indulge in, the matter of the missing jewellery being another. Inevitably, it gave rise to speculation in the pubs at night that, if she persisted, on some night of a full moon, Timmy Cronin, in one of his unpredictable phases, might find her shapely silhouette just too irresistible not to have a pot shot at. In the event, such an unsavoury outcome was averted, when Ellen was prevailed upon to abandon her nocturnal habit.

The men would enter the rear area of the old mansion through a narrow steel gate, and it was when I contemplated that gate clanging shut behind them that I feared for them. For they would

*Sergeant Kelleher in O'Connell Street, Dublin,
in 1923 just before joining the Garda.*

*The Sergeant's old homestead at North Main Street,
Youghal, Co. Cork (centre building).*

The building (centre) that was the barracks in Abbeyleix, where the Sergeant and his family lived before the Catholic clergy had him moved to Pallas.

Sergeant Kelleher together with his wife, who is holding Patrick (author), while older brother Michael is held by his father. The setting is Abbeyleix, from which town the Sergeant was transferred to Pallas for allowing, contrary to Catholic clergy wishes, girls in 'unseemly' dress to dance in the town hall.

*The author (left) with his older brother, Michael,
on the barrack steps in the 1930s.*

*A shot of the tiny village of Pallas in the 1930s,
taken from the roof of Pallas Barracks.*

*Members, their wives and friends of the barracks in happier times in the 1940s.
The author's mother is fourth from the left in the middle row.
His father, the sergeant is kneeling, bottom right.*

*The author at St Fintan's school, Doon, in Co. Limerick
(fourth from left seated in second row) in the early 1940s.*

Dan Duff (centre) at a dance with colleagues and friends in 1945.

The author, Patrick Kelleher, in O'Connell Street, Dublin, after his friend and one-time mentor was released from prison in 1951.

Sergeant Kelleher with his wife (centre) and some members of his family a few years before leaving Pallas in 1957.

The Sergeant's third son, Jimmy (Jamie), with the girls from Cunningham's on a Sunday afternoon in the early 1950s. Cunningham's was a pub, grocery and drapery shop. Jimmy was waiting for a lift to a match.

Pallas Barracks in the 1970s before being shut down.

The author's nephews, David and James, on the steps of the barracks after it had been closed in the 1980s.

Kilduff Castle.

Sarsfield's Rock, a famous landmark near Kilduff, where Patrick Sarsfield waited before torching the siege train in 1690 on its way to Limerick during the Williamite wars.

somehow have to find a means of spending a solid eight hours together, as the regulations required, probably at times with a desire to strangle one another, so fraught was their relationship. And when it was eventually revealed that they had found a rather irregular way of coping, I found it difficult to blame them, for I had been in that gloomy orchard once or twice as a boy, led astray by an enterprising classmate in a few daring raids on the way home from school. With its high walls, it was a place as hard to escape from as it was to enter, and you got a feeling that there was a likelihood of your being trapped inside if someone came upon you unexpectedly. And if that fear gripped us in broad daylight, just imagine what it must have been like for Dan and Byrne, all night with always the possibility that Timmy Cronin was lurking somewhere near.

But Cronin would not have to have a gun. A box of matches, or a lighted cigarette, was all he required, for the hay barns were expected to be his first target. It was a type of arson that was a traditional reminder in the land war days of nastier things to come. And so our two heroes from the barracks, as they hung about, could contemplate any number of possible threats, and could hardly be blamed if sometimes they saw enemies where there were only shadows. Meantime, the joke in the pubs was: 'God help the luckless poacher who pops his head above the proverbial parapet some time after midnight.'

It was, as usual, the old-timers around the village who had lived through the land wars who were the shrewdest judges of what the eventual outcome was likely to be. Their view was that the tension simply could not continue; only a calamity would break the impasse, especially with nerves becoming more and more frayed by the day.

CHAPTER 15

'Insanity,' the writer Fay Weldon, once wrote, in a reference to the 1940s and the 1950s, 'was the great dark fear of the age.' And that now is what came rather too close for comfort in the barracks. It was the worst of all possible times, given the pressure all the gardaí were under. More usually, the officers had to deal with the odd farming lad when, in conditions of social isolation and lack of sympathy within the family for his plight, his behaviour became erratic. If then, in his frustration, he showed the slightest tendency towards anger, he was in grave danger of being deemed potentially violent. And, sadly, this was but a short step away from a committal order being signed and Father and his men summoned, usually in the dead of night, to remove him to the Central Mental Lunatic Asylum on the edge of the city of Limerick.

As youngsters in our quarters in the barracks, we would hear in the night the commotion when men were being manhandled into the cells, to await their removal the following day. We would cover our heads with the bedclothes and, in fear, whisper to one another, 'A lunatic'. We had come to believe, as did many in the village, that such men in their supposed madness could summon up the strength of twelve ordinary men, especially when being dragged from their only sanctuary, their bed and psychological hiding place.

But the men in the barracks would never have anticipated that on a morning after they had carried to its awful conclusion such an order, it could possibly happen to one of them. That, however, was precisely what befell one of their number in the early months of the armed night-duty assignment at Mount Catherine, and it was to send shock waves through the ranks. A new officer was expected to replace Byrne, who was on holiday, and partner Dan on armed duty for a few weeks. Dan had already had his share of ill luck with some of the people he had encountered, and was unfortunate enough yet again to be paired with the latest oddball to arrive in the barracks. With some difficulty he had seen off the Scanlon men who had shown an irrational dislike for him. Then he was detailed to partner Byrne on night duty, who treated him only with contempt, and now came his close encounter with the strangest character of all.

I was in the day room on the afternoon the new man arrived. Hollis, the most unsuitable man in the building to handle such a delicate situation, was barrack orderly that day. I had found him sitting by the phone enveloped in a cloud of smoke, his cigarette held aloft in his immaculately manicured right hand. He was chuckling delightedly to himself as he perused the latest, allegedly salacious, bestseller smuggled to him from London. The previous one I had seen him all but drool over was a bodice-ripper entitled *Forever Amber*. The eponymous Amber, so far as I could judge from the blurb, was once a sixteen-year-old waif on London's streets who rose to become the favourite mistress of Charles II. But on this particular day, Hollis had before him the latest publication that was supposed to have shocked London and elsewhere and which featured a lady by the name of Constance Chatterley who, Hollis explained to me, was stalking the gamekeeper on her crippled husband's estate in search of certain sexual satisfactions not available to her at home. But what gave him such great cause for merriment, it seemed, was that he saw a parallel to that precise situation in, of all places, Mount Catherine. Apparently his two night-duty colleagues had jokingly informed him, knowing his lecherous nature, that as they passed beneath Ellen Kennedy's bedroom window each night, it seemed that she was blatantly defying Cronin's threat by appearing semi-undressed.

Hollis pretended to believe this story. Whereupon, he told me laughingly that, like the fictitious Lady Chatterley, Ellen was a very lonely and frustrated lady and, by her daring appearances behind flimsy curtains, was probably signalling to some lover lurking in the undergrowth that she too was 'ready, willing and able'.

Hollis lived in a fantasy world all his own, and what gave him endless cause for amusement and idle licentious speculation was the notion of a beautiful woman, childless and married into unhappiness, tied to an ageing male and, as a result, ending up, libidinously speaking, as a very frustrated woman indeed. It may be that he saw in such a woman a mirror image of his own loveless existence, symptoms of which were his chain-smoking, his consumption of enormous quantities of porter, late hours in smoke-filled rooms with card-playing cronies, ending up snoring so loudly in the barrack dormitory that sometimes he could be heard downstairs.

I always thought Hollis believed that if the world were made a fairer place, by some divine intervention, he would be brought together with one of these lonely, forty-something females he dreamt about and who would soothe and console him, and she would confirm for him what he saw each morning in his believing mirror: a man unique, flawless and without peer, a bachelor condemned paradoxically, by his own self-evident superiority, to live a lie.

But Hollis's fantasizing ended quite suddenly and the mood in the day room darkened. One minute, convulsed with laughter, he was enjoying the supposedly predatory exploits of beautiful but lonely older women, while the next he was confronted by a giant of a man, the first I had seen tower over him. This individual, who wore a strange and pained expression, bounded into the day room unannounced. For once I saw Hollis ill at ease, facing a man whom he knew immediately was not to be trifled with. The newcomer, not waiting for Hollis's greeting, thrust out his right hand, announcing somewhat gruffly, 'I'm Tom London … Detective Branch.'

The face of the visitor showed all the signs of a misspent youth which had prematurely aged him. He was a sort of Dorian Gray figure—once handsome, once young, but now with a certain dissolute look about him, as well as an angry sadness disfiguring what might well have been a not undistinguished countenance. He was clearly, for whatever reason, suffering greatly, judging by the expression on his face.

I had often heard it said at the station that the branch men were a tough breed, that many lived on the edge and some occasionally went right over it. Hollis's efforts to humour the fellow were having little success, for he was dour and unforthcoming. Impulsively, he picked up a newspaper and pretended to read, so difficult did he appear to find conversation. Hollis introduced me to him as the sergeant's son, but he barely acknowledged me. Studying him as he read, it occurred to me that not only was he on the edge but in grave danger, metaphorically, of making a swift descent into the abyss below.

Father, whose office was nearby, had heard London arrive. He soon bustled in to greet the new man with outstretched hand. But even he was taken aback. It was not merely the detective's sheer physique that intimidated him, but his anguished, contorted face. His attempt to force a smile for Father failed miserably, so he was ushered into his office.

The interview did not last long, for Hollis and I soon heard the pair, as if in some hurry, tramp upstairs and then downstairs again, Father showing London the sleeping quarters and dining area. But, judging by the speed with which Father returned alone, London had shown scant interest in these. Shortly after Father darted into the day room once more, looking bewildered and muttering an expletive as he dashed to the front window, telling Hollis and me, as he went, what had happened.

'That bloody tec', he said angrily, staring towards the crossroads outside, 'has already borrowed my last fiver and my bicycle and I don't know where he's headed.'

Unusually for him, Hollis resisted a jest. Even he and I were beginning to sense that this development was no joking matter, given that London was shortly to be entrusted with a gun, and along with Dan, sent out on night duty, to patrol the enclosed back area of Mount Catherine.

After about an hour London returned. He looked in no better shape. He seemed, however, to be excited about something, if indeed that strained face of his was capable of registering much animation. He looked Hollis in the eye, keen to share something. Fortunately, Dan had just entered and, having been introduced to London, was present to witness the exchange that followed.

'Did you ever notice', London asked Hollis, 'when you go up towards the church that there are four trees in a line on the hill, and when you come back down there are five?'

It was truly a strange question, and when taken together with the man's excited state, deserved, at the very least, a cautious but sensitive response. However, not untypically, Hollis tried to make a joke about it.

'That depends, Tom', he said, laughing heartily, 'on how many pints you had while you were up there.'

It was a near fatal mistake, for the man before him may well have been seeking some reassurance that his, London's, faculties were in full working order, which clearly they were not. Moreover, to add insult to injury, Hollis's reference to drinking made his quip doubly insensitive for he should have noticed the Pioneer pin in London's lapel.

But it was Dan's alertness and uncanny awareness of what was about to happen next that saved the day. For, as London hurriedly left the room, Hollis breathed a sigh of relief. But it was Dan who sensed immediately where London was headed—the press that stored the night-duty men's revolvers in Father's office, London probably having seen them when Father brought him there. Dan leapt after him and managed to slam shut the press in time and remove the key. He had saved Hollis's skin, the same man who had scarpered on the night of the circus, leaving Dan to his fate.

It had been a scary moment, but it confirmed for me that Dan had near psychic powers of foresight. Given that he was still a probationer, however, Hollis would have opportunities to repay him if any difficulty arose for him, but Dan was no fool and probably had already decided that Hollis was not dependable.

Father had now seen enough to know the sort of man he had on his hands. However, he managed to persuade London to lie down for a few hours and get some rest. But when the detective appeared in the dining room later, his mental state was soon revealed. On seeing Christ's image in a picture on the wall, the only religious picture in the building, he prostrated himself, humble before his Maker.

Religious madness, it is said, might result from many causes but could be fuelled especially by deep guilt for some past sins. And so around midnight Father established with a few telephone calls that London was, in effect, returning from a long illness; Garda headquarters believed that he was fully recovered. But when told the nature of the man's affliction, Father knew immediately that, if neglected at the outset, there was no cure. London was a doomed man.

It emerged that, as a very young detective in the 1920s, London found himself patrolling the Dublin quays, the then equivalent of Joyce's 'Nighttown'. And, no doubt blissfully unaware of the dangers, he probably partook all too eagerly of the dubious delights to be found there. Now he faced the terrible consequences, having contracted an affliction which, if neglected, in the end manifested itself in the brain. And so, before nightfall Father did two things in a rather bizarre order. First, he cycled to the church and demanded his fiver from the sacristan, London probably having told him what he had done with it, and then Father phoned a doctor. The medic persuaded London that he be allowed to examine him and he duly confirmed the severe diagnosis. He then delivered to the hapless detective a strong injection and the elephantine London was soon well sedated, making it relatively easy to remove him.

I happened to be in the barrack day room as three of them took him out with heavy hearts, for he was, after all, one of their own. As they escorted him down those treacherous stone steps, I sensed that London was becoming aware of his destination, for he began to struggle.

But there had been an incident in the barracks, a year or so before, even more harrowing than London's. It concerned a somewhat eccentric British army major who had just been demobbed, and who, having heard that Ireland was a tranquil oasis and was known as Ireland of the thousand welcomes, decided to cycle around the island as a sort of therapy after the trauma of war.

One evening, he placed his bicycle against the barn of a farmyard just outside the village and lay down to rest his weary bones. Early the next morning the farmer came upon him sleeping soundly in the hay and addressed him with a cheerful 'Hello'. The fellow failed to respond. The farmer, as he would a sleeping bullock, delivered him a gentle boot in the ribs, whereupon the major awoke swiftly, his alarmed expression indicating that he judged the farmer's action to be inconsistent with the friendliness he had been led to expect in the land of a thousand welcomes.

An old Etonian, his upper-crust accent made his speech unintelligible to the farmer and the farmer's north Munster tones were equally bewildering. As a result, a shouting match developed and soon it was apparent that all communication between the two men was failing. The farmer concluded, given the man's wild-looking expression and eccentric dress, that he was all but demented. Father was sent for but, since he wasn't around, two burly lieutenants of his soon arrived on the scene. And they too were of the opinion that the stranger's bedraggled state and fighting mood did, indeed, indicate that it was unsafe to have him at large. His efforts to explain himself made no sense to them, so they took him forcibly. He was little more than skin and bone. No doctor was available, so, fearing that he might do himself or someone else an injury, one more time that repository for the misunderstood on the edge of the city beckoned. But little did the eccentric major realize that he was fighting his last fight for, no sooner was he inside the gates of the institution than the men in white coats appeared and, without prior medical examination, his backside was bared and a strong injection delivered to him. He expired forthwith.

It was, surely, the cruellest of all possible ironies. Here was a tough little ex-soldier who had come unscathed through the entire war. He had faced Rommel's tanks in the desert and been mentioned in dispatches; he had come through the Italian campaign and entered Rome in triumph with the Allied armies; he had been among the first to scramble ashore on Normandy's beaches on D-Day, and survived that too. And yet he was, in the end, to fall foul of a not intentionally unfriendly farmer in the Ireland of a thousand welcomes he had heard so much about, and to which he had come, in all goodwill and optimism, for what he hoped would be a therapeutic sojourn.

But then, as Dan had been finding out to his cost, Pallas was no health spa, nor was the barracks, by any stretch of the imagination, a therapy clinic.

When the officers returned, having deposited London in the asylum, I could see that they looked shaken by the experience. It was evident that, 'but for the grace of God', it could have been any one of them. And, in particular, it was Dan who made the most revealing remark to me on his return, as he jogged past the cells and up the stairway. It was the first time that he had been called upon to physically remove a man, utterly beyond reason, who was to be his mate on armed duty that very night, and to have him committed, probably for evermore.

I knew Dan had been suffering greatly under the lash of Byrne's abrasive tongue and had seen his love affair with Phoebe Connell under threat from her father's clumsy interference. And his expression that morning showed it all. He stopped on the stairway and, looking me in the eye for little more than a split second, said, almost in a daze, 'It is indeed a fine line, isn't it?'

As he left me, knowing his prescient nature, I wondered if that remark reflected his fear that, some day soon, he might cross that fine line himself.

CHAPTER 16

Phoebe Connell was no highborn maiden, but her father saw her as just that. The colonel seemed to fear that, given her penchant for having as many handsome young men, and some not so young, as she could find at her parties, unless he was ever present and watchful, some local Lothario would slip through the vetting procedure he had devised and impregnate her in the blink of an eye.

Phoebe, you see, was no more than seventeen, but with her tall stature and ample bosom, many were fooled as to her true age. However, men everywhere respond instinctively to a woman who exudes sex appeal and, as a result, young Phoebe had the pick of all personable young men in the locality. And these young guns all but snarled at one another when they arrived on Sunday afternoons, as they competed on entering for the almost indecently passionate embrace she bestowed with equal fervour on each one. But, as we would soon discover, that embrace, to those of us who knew the inside story of the Connell household, had method in its madness.

Lovely Phoebe, however, was fortunate in one other vital respect, for any young ladies locally who might have even remotely approached her allure had long since been dispatched to convents all over the country, the express motivation for such banishment being to secure for them a good education. But, at a more unconscious level, it may well have been to ensure that, for as long as possible, they retained that blessed gift known as virginity. It was hoped they would avoid the fate of the less privileged in the village and surrounding area who, in their teens, found themselves with child and were forced, in shame and secrecy, to undertake a bitter journey across the sea to sleazy clinics in the back streets of alien English cities. And, given the shame these girls brought upon themselves and their families, the attitude locally appeared to have been, 'Who the hell cares?'

And so the young men Phoebe favoured with an invitation arrived one by one at the appointed hour on Sunday afternoons fresh-faced and eager, while those not so favoured gathered at the crossroads, a stone's throw from her vast drawing-room window from which echoed music, laughter and song. And it was there, almost within earshot, that lovely Phoebe's verbal deflowering proceeded apace.

As it did, every vile innuendo in the book was flung about at the crossroads, to loud guffaws to drag her down, all deemed to be justified by her daring to entertain more than one young man at a time, a sign surely that she had become a young girl of very easy virtue indeed. Many in their hearts dissented, but went along with the easy hilarity of crossroads humour.

But there was a huge irony there too, for though the young gallants languishing outside may have been at the least envious, most of those admitted to the colonel's house were deluded. For they were being used as an elaborate smokescreen, to prevent her father from identifying Phoebe's true love. And he was Dan, from the barracks, with the sensuous brooding visage of a poet, magnificent luminous eyes, the singing voice unmatched in the locality and a way with words that made young ladies swoon.

Participating in this ruse to fool the colonel, in sympathy as they were with Phoebe's deep passion for her man, were none other than her mother and older sister. And how they enjoyed seeing the old gaffer perplexed, pretending, as they did, that it was the wish of Phoebe's older and less attractive sister that the young policeman be invited.

At that time, courtship in rural Ireland was something of an obstacle race. True, marriage and family were respectable institutions, always provided that, in the eyes of mother church, an excess of sexual pleasure was not derived therefrom: but romance and courtship outside wedlock were deeply frowned upon.

Ironically, in penal times the hapless Roman clergy were driven into the fields and hedges to celebrate what was most dear to them—the sacraments; now the wheel had come full circle, and it was into those same fields and hedges that young men and women were driven, in their turn, to celebrate that which was most dear to them: passion for one another. And it was those zealous men in black, with white collars, once themselves a hunted species, but now very much in the ascendant, who visited upon these young lovers the same repression that they themselves had suffered all those years before.

For, on Sunday nights, certain of the more fanatical of these clerical gentlemen rampaged abroad with blackthorn sticks at the ready, apoplectic with rage on seeing human forms lying together in semi-darkness and seemingly ardent embraces, deep in the lush roadside hedges.

Company-keeping, as it was known, was deeply suspect, and when indulged in secretly and with apparently lubricious satisfaction, was to these zealous churchmen anathema, sinful in mortal dimension, almost beyond forgiveness. In their fury, these

angry men of God poked their blackthorns into the vague outlines
of entwined bodies, such satanic nocturnal interventions giving,
surely, a whole new meaning to the notion of contraception.

I shall always remember when I first came upon these love lairs
by the side of the narrow overgrown roadway when, with my
friends, we made our way to school on Monday mornings. We
would stop suddenly on seeing one of these deep indentations
in the rich hedges, and quietly wonder if some sort of monster
had lain there. Having stared at them for a long time, trying
to fathom their origin, eventually, with puberty beckoning, it
dawned on us what they signified. Thus, the so-called facts of
life were made known to us, not by parents or teachers, but by
nature herself. And then anxious and upset for reasons we knew
not, and unable to communicate our thoughts to one another,
we hurried silently to school.

These were, of course, uncomfortable places for young lovers
to release their pent-up passion for one another, but they had
at least the virtue of a degree of privacy. Yet that advantage was
denied Phoebe Connell for she was forced to entertain her lover
and other guests in the glare of her well-lit drawing room, under
her father's persistent gaze. She could not allow herself even a
touch of the youth's hand in case she betrayed his identity.

But the ruse to fool the colonel backfired on Phoebe in one
important respect. For those uninvited young men languishing at
the crossroads had ensured, through their malicious gossip, that
her reputation would be severely undermined, leaving some doubt
in the village that she was any longer the chaste young lady she was
supposed to be. And, of all places, it was in the barrack day room,
with her man present, that in the course of a bizarre incident her
supposed promiscuity was raised obliquely in conversation.

A card game was in session when a charming young man in his early thirties entered. By name Seán, he came from a well-known entrepreneurial family from Dromkeen, a couple of miles from Pallas. He seemed slightly inebriated and he carried a very small suitcase. Known well to the older members of the station, though not a regular visitor, he was dressed immaculately in a magnificent tweed overcoat, with exquisite suit, shirt and tie, and stylish trilby hat. He resembled Gene Kelly, and was ready to dance, sing, play cards or do anything required of him to entertain us, as long as he was granted the very special request for which he had come. He told us that he was just back from the White City greyhound racetrack in London and hinted that his journey had indeed been well worth it. And then, hardly pausing for breath, he launched into an explanation of the purpose of his visit to the barracks.

'I hear', he said smiling, conspiratorially, 'that young Phoebe Connell, across the way, is a gamey lass and I thought you fellows might arrange an invitation for me to one of her parties.'

There was a sharp intake of breath around the room for the rest of us knew of Dan's relationship with Phoebe, and that this man's remark was grossly out of order. By my side, I noted Dan's body tense and I saw his left hand clenching and unclenching. I had seen that left hand lash out to lethal effect on the infamous night of the circus, and wondered for a moment if I would shortly see our visitor's smug countenance on the receiving end.

But Hollis intervened quickly to avert what could have been a nasty incident. 'I presume, Seán', he said sarcastically, 'that, as always, your intentions are honourable?'

Hollis's swift riposte found its mark and the visitor, knowing he had blundered, looked deflated. Whereupon Dan rose and, excusing himself, left the room. With that, the visitor regained his composure and his confident smile returned. He was well known locally as a playboy, a cynical predator on young farm maids, and his brazen request ran true to form. He may have consumed some alcohol, but he was drunk with more than that, with the arrogant belief that he was the answer to every woman's prayer. And so he proceeded to reveal the purpose of his suitcase while we waited, intrigued to discover what on earth it could contain to further his goal which was, of course, to seduce the colonel's daughter.

But the visitor did not use those words. Instead, he told us he was about to prove how he was best equipped to 'show Phoebe a good time', a euphemism for his more dastardly intentions. His hands hovered over the little case, as if he was a magician who, for our enlightenment and entertainment, would produce a white rabbit from it.

We watched and waited expectantly, barely suppressing laughter, as the tension mounted. We knew the visitor was a trickster to his fingertips and would make some amazing revelation. Having already removed his coat and hat, and hung them with the police batons on the wall, he took off his jacket and tie. But it was when he went one step further, and untied his trouser belt, that we feared the worst.

There was, you see, a story oft told around the village about a local world-beating weight thrower who, in his day, had flung the thing all over America to record distances, but never succeeded in doing so under the national flag, which would have won him an Olympic gold for his native land. This man, to the consternation of the most hardened drinking men in Cunningham's, once performed, after a few drinks, a trick he had learnt in the saloon bars of Chicago—placing nakedly on the bar counter, to prove his superior virility, a vital part of his anatomy.

But mercifully our visitor stopped short of such a fearsome spectacle, his belt-loosening intended merely to facilitate the removal of his shirt. As he lifted it over his head, ever so carefully, there was a gasp around the room at the sight now revealed. He noted with immense satisfaction our bemusement and laughter. Then he posed us a question: 'How many pairs of ladies' nylons, fellows,' he asked, 'would you say there are strapped around my shoulders?'

The question was a serious one for, among his many other nefarious activities, this man was a small-time smuggler and, in those frugal post-war years, his entrepreneurial flair and devil-may-care personality were as much admired and applauded in the barracks as anywhere locally. Rather like a corrupt politician, his combination of brass neck and manic humour enabled him to top the popularity stakes among his male peers, while the females, given the patriarchal nature of our society, were forced, silently, to acquiesce.

Meantime the young farm girls he had dishonoured could no longer show their faces in the neighbourhood, for while he was admired for his daring, panache and success with the opposite sex, the same was not true for them. All the world, as they say, loves a lover, but no one loves a slut! And so this man would be free for many a year afterwards to roam his happy hunting ground in and around Pallas, splashing out his ill-gotten gains which would enable him to purchase the virtue of almost any young girl gullible enough, especially when in the throes of passion, to believe that she would be loved and cherished by him for evermore.

And so, having gleefully demonstrated his belief that the true test of a man's womanizing successes is the size of his wallet, he told us that he would gain tenfold for every single pair of the several hundred nylons he had brought in. It was then we saw the purpose of the little case as, unabashed, he removed each pair lovingly from his shoulders and placed them ever so gently in the suitcase. As we watched, we knew in our hearts that, in these various activities, his political connections in east Limerick, as well as his friendships in the barracks, would do him no harm. Implicit in his demeanour and bizarre presentation was, of course, the notion that he was, of all who so aspired, the one best equipped to have his wicked way with Phoebe Connell, but thankfully he was denied. And there was a release of tension and quiet satisfaction in the day room to see him, deflated, depart with Hollis for a sort of consolation prize, a jolly booze-up in Cunningham's. Here, we knew, Hollis would no doubt explain to him that, while his deep desire for Phoebe was well understood, the lady in question was spoken for.

Dan and I departed for Phoebe's party. I was apprehensive as we entered the upstairs drawing room, for the rumour around the village was that Colonel Connell had somehow tumbled to the fact that it was the man I was accompanying, the penniless recruit, with whom his beautiful young daughter was besotted. It was rumoured further, if not common knowledge, that it was in darkness behind the massive wooden barrack gates that Phoebe and her man's love trysts took place. They were engineered by Phoebe herself, it seems, for she managed to ensure that she had each evening a letter to post, and on her return the couple slipped inside the gate for a swift and reassuring embrace, sometimes, no doubt, all the more passionate for the haste and secrecy forced upon them.

But one evening Phoebe returned home in a dishevelled state, passion having, presumably, reached close to climactic levels. On seeing her, the colonel flew into a rage. Phoebe, it was said, coolly blamed the wind and rain, but the colonel was no fool and the fear was that he was biding his time until the next party evening.

As we came in, the drawing room was pulsating with music, animated conversation and laughter, while an unknown youngster prepared to strike up on his melodeon. But there was, I detected, as always when the colonel was present, an underlying tension, for the man was socially awkward and innately suspicious. Indeed, it was as if he had never quite removed his army uniform, for it seemed that he desired to be in absolute control of the proceedings and every now and then he rose from his chair, inscrutable of face, and tramped up and down the room. And, in that mood, I knew from experience, almost anything could happen.

Yet the party went well, at least at the start. Phoebe, at the piano, was surrounded by fawning young men, each desperately seeking some sign that he was the chosen one. Several acted their parts on the stage, some with songs, others with recitations and one or two with musical instruments. But it was only when Dan was called upon and obliged that the room went quiet with appreciation, so extraordinary was that tenor voice.

Each time he sang, Phoebe accompanied him. Towards the end of the evening he treated us to his favourite, 'Lili Marlene'. Before he finished, however, the colonel gave an ominous sign of what was to come. Rising from his chair before Dan had finished, he gave only the most perfunctory, almost derisive, applause, while loud approval from the rest of us resounded around the room.

Swept away by the emotion of the moment, Phoebe made an error of impulsiveness that she would live to regret. Jumping up excitedly, as teenagers will, with all the impetuosity of extreme youth, she threw her arms around her man. The colonel glared at the pair in anger mixed with dismay, for it had proven to him what he may well have suspected—that it was indeed the police recruit, too clever by half to be trusted, to whom Phoebe had given her heart.

When she saw the colonel glaring at her, her tears began to flow. She grabbed Dan's hand and they left the room abruptly, the assembled gathering clearing a path for them as they went. Some minutes later, the colonel all but kicked some chairs aside and, to his shame, departed in pursuit of the pair as they disappeared downstairs.

The rest of us, gobsmacked by this turn of events, said our thanks and goodbyes to Phoebe's mother and older sister and departed. Curiosity burnt inside us, however, for we knew there was high drama downstairs and we left reluctantly, but there was no doubt where our sympathies lay.

It was several days before the full story emerged, insofar as a full story ever does. It appears that the colonel blundered in on the couple to find them in a passionate embrace in, of all unromantic places, the pantry. Phoebe's tears at this point became uncontrollable and she fled to her room. Whereupon the colonel and Dan faced one another.

'My young man,' the colonel said, 'how do you propose on your police recruit's income to give my daughter the standard of living to which she is accustomed?'

'That, Colonel,' Dan answered coolly, 'is our business, Phoebe's and mine.' At this point Dan made to go, but the colonel, still very angry, posed another extraordinary question. 'And, by the way, do you not know the origin of that last song you sang?'

'It's a song of the war.'

'It's more than that, my young man,' the colonel continued angrily, 'and I should know because I served in two world wars. It's a song a soldier sings at the barrack gate on the night before he goes to war and he sings it to his whore.'

Each day, thereafter, I could see Phoebe at her upstairs window looking pale and distraught. In her distress, she had ever since confined herself to her room, spending most of her waking hours gazing across at the barracks, longing for a sight of Dan.

Sometimes, as I watched, my own feelings were confused, so unhappy did she look. And sometimes I fancied that I saw those beautiful lips I once foolishly spurned were moving, and wondered what words they were uttering. So young and so beautiful and yet so unhappy, she could have been Juliet on her balcony in Verona, and who could say, but the words were Juliet's too, for none other would be more appropriate, 'O Romeo, Romeo! wherefore art thou, Romeo?'

Alas, her Romeo had then serious matters to occupy his mind. For there had been a dramatic development in the Mount Catherine land row, and, as a result, that morning the Kennedys had come in a state of near panic to the station, bringing with them a package that had been delivered in the post. When they opened it, the chilling contents and terse message must have made their blood run cold. The anonymous missive, it was believed, could have come only from Timmy Cronin, back on the warpath after spending three months bound to the peace. But it was the crudely written message that alarmed Father, for implicit therein was the threat that Cronin not only had the Kennedy couple in his gunsights, but their two protectors as well.

It was an alarming development. It had been bad enough for Dan already, his honour compromised by all that had happened, his love thwarted, with perhaps fear in his heart that his very sanity would not hold, and now this.

I had felt since our first meeting, when he had hinted to me that he believed his fate was determined, that it must be an awesome burden to carry around with him. And how those fears must have been reinforced by this latest incident, over which he had no control.

It struck me at the time that most of us in such a dire situation would simply exercise our free will and walk away from it all. But, for Dan, free will did not seem to come into the reckoning. He was, it appeared, set on a course from which there was no turning back, as if he was powerless to influence whatever fate awaited him, and must go blindly onwards, come what may.

CHAPTER 17

It was customary at the time, when guests invited to a wedding were unable to attend, to send them in the post some time later pieces of that elaborate confection known as wedding cake. These little morsels, from the happy couple's table, were duly packed in tiny cardboard boxes with little silver bells on top and the whole wrapped with pink ribbons.

It was such an innocent-looking parcel that was delivered to Mount Catherine House, and it was a rather bemused postman who said, when questioned later, that while he had in his day delivered many such little boxes, this one had intrigued him most because its contents rattled.

And so the Kennedys, though not remembering any recent wedding invitation, were pleased and repaired to the rear of the building and requested from a servant an early cup of tea. Quite a shock was in store for them, however, for when they unwrapped the parcel, they discovered four deadly little pointed objects as far removed from being edible as anything could possibly be. And though the Kennedys dabbled in antiques and suchlike, *objets d'art* they most certainly were not. In fact, in criminal underworld terminology they were known as 'slugs'.

The constituent parts of this package lay on Father's desk at the barracks one afternoon as Hollis, McCabe and I gathered round him, staring in silent fascination, mixed with horror, at the lethal display. Father was reflective for a long time, knowing doubtlessly that those of us looking on did not have enough gravitas between us to engage him with any seriousness on this worrying development. But it was clear to us that this meant that Cronin, in a most unexpected and chilling manner, had decided to remind the Kennedys that his patience with them was running out.

Father, after poking at the exhibit for a while with his long, slender, silver letter-opener, finally delivered himself of a rather deadly summing up. 'Four little killers,' he said, uttering the words through his teeth as if to himself. He allowed the phrase to echo in the air before showing a rare philosophical side to his thinking: 'The one saving grace, I suppose, is that the manner of the presentation of these ugly things, in wedding-cake packaging no less, might well indicate that Timmy, despite everything, may have a sense of humour.'

The bullets were squat and ugly, bronze in colour, and they had already been removed from their coffin-shaped box, a small cardboard container. They were still on their tiny layer of brown straw. Beside them was a little card on which were scrawled the spine-tingling words 'One for each', and it was to this deadly message that Father then turned his attention.

He studied the writing, comparing it for a long moment with the name and address label on the wrapper, obviously trying to determine if both had been written by the same hand. He did not comment, however, on the significance of those ominous words, probably for the very reason that the possible implications were too awful for idle speculation and should be left to the imagination. For the said words obviously meant that not only were the Kennedy pair in Cronin's gunsights, but also the two officers, Duff and Byrne, sleeping just overhead and no doubt exhausted in mind and body after many months of night duty, which must have felt a sort of living hell. And it was Father's unenviable duty to apprise them, as soon as they awoke, of that sinister, three-word message.

And so, for a time, we observed an unprompted and respectful silence, mindful that the men sleeping above were Father's colleagues. Predictably enough, it was the incorrigible Hollis, a man who could never endure solemnity for long, who rudely interrupted our worried reflections. Deciding, as usual, to lighten the prevailing mood, whenever it bordered on the grave, he searched his frivolous brain for a comic, if not licentious, angle to the display of deadly ordinance before us.

'Sarge,' he said, 'what these little things remind me of are the wizened penises of dead pygmies you would see in the souvenir shops in remotest Africa.'

Father threw his eyes up to heaven. He never responded to Hollis's jesting, for if he had done, just once, the barracks might have assumed the atmosphere of a comedy theatre. Instead, he turned to McCabe. 'Mac,' he said, 'will you put on some gloves, wrap up this stuff and send it to the forensic people.'

McCabe offered no comment throughout, nor did he answer Father or look him in the eye. McCabe never looked anyone in the eye if he could avoid it, fearing presumably that the truth about the inner man was to be found there. McCabe's one saving grace was that he was a very efficient administrator and, on being instructed, he bent briskly to his task.

I was always uneasy in McCabe's presence, ever since Father, without explanation, told me one afternoon, several years before, to release the air out of my bicycle tyres when McCabe invited me to the cinema. He did not trust McCabe, given his reputation for seeking out the company of young boys. But, at the same time, Father did not want me to decline his invitation without explanation. Father, I came to believe, had to tread warily with him, for it was known that McCabe had friends in high places, presumably of like mind and inclination, who would ensure that a finger was never laid on him.

It was often said that sergeants had more problems inside than outside their stations, and nowhere was it more true than in Pallas. Not long before Father had found a drunken Hollis *in flagrante delicto* with the ageing barrack cook, the wretched woman pinned under the mountainous Hollis on the hard mattress that overlay a cold, steel frame which passed in the barracks for a bed. To this profoundly unerotic spectacle, Father had no option but to turn a blind eye, an eye so accustomed to being averted from many unsavoury incidents in the barracks that it would not have surprised me if he had suffered some permanent diminishment of that particular faculty.

Before we departed, Father looked for a long moment out of his office window, deep in thought, as he contemplated the far Slieve Phelim hills. I followed his gaze, and wondered if he was seeking inspiration from that gully in the hills, which he had often pointed out to me, down which Patrick Sarsfield rode on his way to blowing up the Williamite siege trains at nearby Ballineety in 1690. It was unlikely, however, that Sarsfield would have tolerated deadwood in his ranks for as long as Father was forced to do.

That afternoon Father looked gloomier than I had ever seen him, as he watched McCabe with gloved hands finishing his task of putting into tiny linen bags the four key items of the lethal package. I took one final look at them, those brutal little objects of death, before they were taken away. And I recoiled at the thought that that one of those could, in an instant, extinguish the life of my good friend sleeping upstairs, not to speak of another one penetrating deep into the still shapely torso of Ellen Kennedy.

Father led us out. McCabe left last, being a man who, for a variety of reasons, had to watch his back, fearful that a metaphorical dagger might some day be plunged in it, especially if a cock-up were to happen in the handling of the land row, and a scapegoat sought. In that event, however, not only McCabe, but the entire barracks contingent could be swept away to dead-end stations all over the country.

Hollis never entertained such negative thoughts, and went out of Father's office in his customary jaunty way, pushing his peak cap farther back on his head clown-like, as he went in search of someone who might see the funny side of all this. And, if it turned out to be the ebullient barrack cook herself, then so it would have to be.

But laughter anywhere in the building was a scarce commodity in those difficult days. The nearest Byrne ever came to merriment, even in response to Hollis's joking, was to clear his throat even more aggressively, while Dan drifted about increasingly serious and brooding, as if he too, like Hamlet, had lost a father, murderously, and could not make up his mind what to do about it.

But what was perplexing everyone in the village was not the gravity of the atmosphere in the barracks and the precarious state of relationships there, of which complexities they knew little, but what in God's name, had possessed Timmy Cronin, at this stage of his campaign, to reach for the gun? Many of the older villagers knew from the land war days that a plethora of less lethal options was available to him to try to get the Kennedys to see sense. He might, for example, have simply tossed a lump of poison over a hedge late some evening and a whole paddock-full of valuable horseflesh would soon be laid low, or smashed down a few strategically chosen fences and in no time the precious animals would be roaming the countryside. Or, most favoured of all in the old land war days, he could so easily, some dark night, have tossed a lighted cigarette butt into a haybarn and watched with glee, from afar, the resultant conflagration. But the gun: surely that was always a last resort?

One way or another, however, Cronin had now heaped the pressure on all concerned. It showed first on the Kennedys, who had gone to ground, not showing up at Mass or at other engagements. Meantime, Father and the superintendent were more at loggerheads than ever, the latter making Father see red with the suggestion that Dan should be transferred to another station because it was clear to everybody that his health was suffering from the night duty, while the super's pal, Byrne, remained *in situ*. This would, of course, have prompted Dan to believe that he was to be the fall guy, sacrificed at the whim of a bullying partner. It would be tantamount to demotion for him and deeply hurtful to his pride. How much more, I wondered, could my young friend stomach.

But, ironically, it was upon himself that Cronin had laid the most immense pressure of all. To them he had in a way made a promise, for the deadly threat against the Kennedys was assumed by everyone to have come from him; for now the men with whom he associated expected him to act or he would have no credibility among his friends who wanted to see Kennedy receive his comeuppance.

There were now in the barracks new and serious repercussions, and not solely in the relationship of Father and the superintendent.

The mooted removal of Dan, forthwith, marked a new low, many said, in Machiavellian skulduggery; and it plumbed the depths, if lower depths were possible, in the relationship of Byrne and his all but ostracized young partner. Their antipathy towards one another had largely been covert before that; now it was emerging as open warfare. Fierce clashes they may have had in the past in the dead of night, in the dark, bleak high-walled back garden of Mount Catherine and yet they returned to barracks sometimes even on speaking terms. But now, of all places, confrontation had blown up in the dormitory, with the normally deeply slumbering Hollis awakened by its ferocity.

It was started by a tired, angry Byrne as he undressed for bed: 'You'll have to be on time in future for duty,' he spat out at his no doubt equally tired colleague.

'I'm not afraid of duty. I could get used to night duty anywhere,' Dan replied.

'Well, it's taking you a long time getting used to it here.'

'Listen, if you don't stop nagging me, I'll give you a slap in the mouth.'

'Well, try it on and I'll blow your brains out.'

It was unfair of Byrne to charge Dan with being late, for it was well known that he himself had often been delayed. However, the focus around the village was not now on this internecine conflict, but very much on the anticipated showdown shortly expected at Mount Catherine. Half a century before the tiny village had been torn apart by the land-war agitation involving shootings, evictions and burnings, with the police often caught in the crossfire. Must they, many of the villagers asked, go through something like that again? For, at that time newshounds would swarm around when a killing or any serious incident occurred, seeking a story from someone who could drag a place like Pallas down in the gutter. One famous London journalist went so far as to describe the local people as the most sullen he had encountered in all his travels. The wounds from that era of land-war agitation still ran deep.

And so the days and weeks to follow were awaited with growing apprehension. The old-timers took the view that the Mount Catherine affair was now on a collision course, with little chance of a compromise being reached. Many of the older men were resigned, a state of mind that seemed common to those long-suffering individuals who had been involved not only in the land wars, but in the Troubles and, later still, the horrific Civil War.

True, the majority were law-abiding people who recoiled from any conflict, and the older women worked their beads relentlessly, asking the 'Lord and His Blessed Mother' to intervene in the dreadful Mount Catherine affair. They hoped that, with such divine intervention, the crisis would soon blow over, while being aware, at the same time, that land rows were never that easily resolved.

In Pallas there were also a handful of superstitious folk who insisted that what made some bloodletting inevitable was the fact that Timmy Cronin had never been the full shilling. It was rumoured that, in his younger days, he would roam the fields on the night of a full moon and, in dreadful anguish, holler to high heaven, a sound, they said, that was more spine-chilling than that of the banshee herself. Father, however, knew the fellow better than most and when he heard this sort of talk, he would laugh scornfully at the absurdity of it.

But with such a cosmic phenomenon due that very weekend, an expectation of a calamity of some sort happening was in the air. It was the sort of atmosphere that had not only the old ladies of the village fervently praying, but at home Mother led us in the rosary at bedtime and expressed the hope that, whatever happened that night, no one would be hurt.

CHAPTER 18

Dan may have been no more than a burgeoning young poet, albeit one trapped in a policeman's uniform, but all the signs now were that he was a man in the grip of an obsession. He had, it seemed, one thought alone occupying his fevered brain, one fixation of mind, and that was how to extract himself from the intolerable situation in which he had become enmeshed.

I had known for some time from the remarks he'd made about his future that he may have had a fatalistic streak to his nature, and with each passing day I became more and more convinced. It was a phenomenon I did not fully understand, a sort of death wish maybe, like many say had possessed those brave poets of 1916, Plunkett, Pearse, and MacDonagh. And yet he seemed to have prepared himself, at least physically, to defy that very fate itself. It was a seeming contradiction—to wish to die, yet to strive to stay alive.

It may well be that these morbid fears had dogged him all his life. How grimly ironic, then, that no sooner had he taken up his first posting as a young police officer than the men who fate chose to attempt to maim him, if not to bury him, were, of all professions, undertakers. I looked on, frozen to the spot, that unforgettable night when in semi-darkness no fewer than five of them launched themselves upon him. As they did so, he found himself with his back to a gloomy, semi-abandoned Protestant graveyard. The symbolism of finding himself under deadly physical attack in such a place by such men was not, I felt sure, lost on him. For he was already plagued by morbid fears that he was fated for an early departure to that undiscovered country from whose bourne no traveller returns. It must have been for him, faced by such men in such a place, the worst of all omens, confirming the worst of his fears.

But, in the event, he seemed undaunted and, adopting swiftly a defensive pose, he proceeded to defend himself like a man possessed. In quick order he disposed of one deluded idiot after another until the gravedigger, a pathetic little veteran of the Somme, offered himself as a final sacrificial lamb. He too was felled. One moment Dan's attackers were like ghostly vultures circling for the kill, the next bloody fools lying prostrate in the lush grass, their absurdly long funeral greatcoats draping them like shrouds. It had been a one-man rout.

Dan's defensive skills had served him well that night, but since then the threats, which were coming from closer to home, were subtler, more insidious and psychologically undermining. One such was viewed with dismay by a female pub owner, a former teacher and Dan's literary soulmate, in Coffey's Bar just across from the rear of the barracks.

The hapless superintendent, of all people, a priggish little man who seemed to be permanently on the run from his irascible wife, looked in, no doubt dying for a quick alcoholic fix. He darted a glance about the bar, hoping that, at that particular hour of day, it would be empty. He saw only one customer, his young off-duty junior, whom he well knew was distressed from prolonged night duty, and he was not man enough to join the youngster at the bar and stand him a drink. Instead, turning rapidly on his heels, he blurted out perhaps the unkindest cut of all: 'Oh, it's you,' he said, before departing as furtively as he had come. Miss Coffey reported afterwards that she never in all her life witnessed such cruel indifference to the plight of a young man who had a short time earlier told her 'I fear something is going to happen to me.'

Dan's dilemma was how to deal with this fear, for, given hurt after hurt, betrayal after betrayal, unless he could somehow diffuse the frustration that was building up inside him, he might have found himself plunged into a deeper hell. He was being pushed to the very limits and, if he allowed that to continue, something deep within him would have to give.

The village had noticed the change that had come over him since that first day, about two years before, when we saw him, a handsome, seemingly carefree young man strolling slowly up the village from the afternoon train, pushing before him his old bicycle, on the carrier of which a battered suitcase jockeyed about, as if empty. He had clearly nothing to declare but his youth, his extraordinary level of physical fitness and, as we noted when he came close up, his alertness, an almost pathological level of mental acuity that showed in his eyes.

It was the first time he had set foot in the Golden Vale, and the glorious greenery and pleasant setting of the village, surrounded by hills, seemed to captivate him, for he stopped every so often to gaze across the fields over the railway embankment, before he came to the village proper. He seemed at times, so long did he gaze, almost hypnotized, as if, in his first posting, he felt he had found paradise.

Those of us long accustomed to these topographical features, however, took them for granted, but Dan was no doubt enchanted.

For when life is good for such a man, he sees only the beautiful and the sublime. But now, alas, just two years later, it seemed he saw only treachery lurking all about. Now he saw, one might say, the dark side of paradise; faster than is imaginable, great rapture is often replaced by unrelenting melancholy, in men and women possessed of his rare sensibility.

His failure, however, was that he had been perhaps too passive in the face of tyranny. But, if he had lived a century before, there would have been a solution. It was called duelling. Back then, one simply invited one's tormentor to a quiet hillside at dawn, chose weapons, and the solution came fast and furious, usually out of the muzzle of a gun. To the cult of duelling the law turned a blind eye, for the courts then offered no solution with anything like the finality of the duelling pistol. Whether one lived or died, one's honour was vindicated.

Dan did not have such an option and must sometimes have wished he had. When he came first, he regaled me with stories and poems of men who wrote about such things: Robert Service, Rudyard Kipling, Jack London. There were stories about death in defence of honour, in duels formal and informal. He told me too of the great literary men who, finding their honour besmirched, issued challenges to a duel and sometimes they too were so challenged. He spoke of the quarrel between two great Russians, Tolstoy and Turgenev, when the offended one, Tolstoy, offered his friend that ultimate resolution, but happily for the future of world literature, a reconciliation was effected in time. And he recounted for me also how the great German writer Thomas Mann had a character in his powerful novel *The Magic Mountain* make himself available for a duel on the inevitable snowy hillside at dawn, soon to find the snow between his feet crimson with his own blood, for, unable to find it in his heart to kill another man, he had turned the weapon on himself.

But if my friend had one hero among all those famous literary men and women, it was that other Russian, Pushkin. The great poet was humiliated at the court of the Czar when a French officer there became infatuated with his beautiful wife, Natalie, going so far as to marry her sister to be near her. A duel to the death seemed inevitable. The Frenchman ran from the challenge for a while, but when it finally came, he faced it, alas, breaking not once, but twice, the time-honoured rules of duelling. Pushkin died soon afterwards from his wounds. Russia went into prolonged mourning.

I sometimes fancied, from the passion with which my friend recounted for me that story, that he saw a parallel of sorts with his own situation. He, like Pushkin, suffered daily humiliation at the hands of a colleague in that other court of a kind—the barracks. He too shared with the great poet at least something of his giftedness, but also his vulnerability, and would, I felt sure, if the cult of duelling were still in vogue, have embraced it hungrily, as a way out of his dire predicament.

But he had to look elsewhere for a resolution to his suffering. And, I came to believe, he had to look to nature herself, for when a man is burdened with catastrophic fear, defined by psychiatrists Michael Corry and Áine Tubridy as 'fear that all one holds dear is threatened and one cannot any longer defend it', then nature alone has the answer. It is called the fight or flight imperative. It's as old as history itself and is said to have been programmed into us when we were reptilian creatures of the deep. And that meant simply that Dan now had to choose. No longer could he afford to turn the other cheek. That way, students of such matters know, lies descent into the ultimate abyss—insanity. Besides, no self-respecting reptile of the deep ever did such a thing. The very thought would have made Darwin spin in his grave, if not take flight out of it. So my friend had to confront or depart.

True, many said that fleeing simply compounded a man's agony and possibly left him scarred for life, and that facing up to and boldly facing his tormentor was the only effective option if his dignity and honour were to be restored.

But I believed then that there was another course, a variation one might say on nature's imperative. It would have been for Dan, if taken, a noble course, for it would have encompassed an act of love. It is known as elopement. No shame would have attached to it, for it has been approved and applauded down the ages. For love, is it not always said, conquers all?

In other words, Dan had to take Phoebe Connell and go in the night. For she too desperately sought a way out of her particular hell and, more than that, she needed love, which in the end is the only thing worth having in this crazy world.

Indeed, sudden departures from one sort of tyranny or another were commonplace around Pallas then and metaphors from the war abounded to describe them: abandoning ship, heading for the hills, running for cover, and that most often used in the barracks because of its high risk implication, baling out, the resort of many a hung-over officer, to the amusement of his colleagues, when attempting to dodge a top brass inspection.

But some sudden departures from the village had a slightly bizarre context, and many of these were still talked about in the pubs from time to time. One young police recruit, a few years before, had sought to depart at dawn following a broken love affair, but Father, hearing him drag his heavy trunk down the naked stairway in the night, waylaid him in the yard outside, jumped into his car beside him and instructed him to drive to the lady's residence which happened to be a licensed premises. The party, it was said, went on well beyond daylight.

Often told, too, was the story of the returning emigrant who had made good. He bought a pub and a farm, made a poor fist of the farm and became the best customer of the bar. As matters went downhill, he proceeded to tyrannize his young adult family and, as a result, his daughter ran off with a clown from the circus, his eldest son headed for England, taking two hundred head of cattle with him, while the second son simply disappeared.

But the departure that provided the greatest hilarity in the village was the story of the dapper little railway porter who cuckolded the ageing stationmaster. It was apparently a rather secret affair until one day an inebriated farmer, passing through the ticket office at the station, blurted out the unfortunate news to the station master: 'Has no one told you, me man, that that little fucker with the flag outside has been "carrying on" with your wife?' Whereupon, the hapless stationmaster dashed out to the platform brandishing his penknife, leaving the lustful porter no option but to jump aboard the moving train, taking his little green flag with him, never to be seen again in the area. And so, departure for good reason in Pallas was commonplace, and more often than not approved and applauded.

In the world of make-believe, however, in Hollywood say, a more dramatic denouement would have to be devised. Very probably, as a representative of law and order, Dan would be made to confront Cronin some night on the farm, and there would be a swift and bloody resolution to the Mount Catherine affair once and for all, with no prizes for guessing who rode off into the sunset with his lady in tow.

But, alas, this was the real world and a nasty world it was. And there were no pat answers to these problems. In this particular world the chips had to lie the way they fell.

So, despite his fears, I came to believe that Dan would stand and fight. Backing down was not in his nature.

CHAPTER 19

The night was foul. Dark clouds, driven by high winds, swept across the sky. Meantime, the massive oak and beech trees surrounding the old churchyard opposite groaned, tormented by the raging storm. One fierce wind-gust tolled eerily the semi-derelict church bell. 'It's an ill omen,' villagers said.

But it wasn't the only sign of trouble brewing that night. For, most unusually for him in such conditions, Father, in the early evening, was seen to cycle away from the stricken village, uphill and into the teeth of the wind and driving rain. He was red in the face, as if in high dudgeon about some matter in the barracks. It was well known that the superintendent had pulled rank on him yet again over the deployment of the night-duty men at Mount Catherine. And if, as was rumoured, Timmy Cronin had decided to make trouble that very night, I was not surprised that, with all power to influence events stripped from him, Father decided that he was better off out of there.

But the talk of the village that evening was not of my father's strained and seemingly hurried departure, but about the weird ringing of the old church bell, stung, as it were, into protest at the mutinous elements, for the last time such a phenomenon had occurred, the village was plunged into tragedy shortly afterwards. Yet almost any strange sound, especially at night, emanating from that gloomy, alien burial ground tended to cause local people to shiver as they passed by. Unfamiliarity sometimes breeds fear and suspicion, and very few villagers, on pain of eternal damnation, even for a Protestant neighbour's funeral, had ever set foot inside those high, forbidding steel gates, darkened by overhanging trees; and, as if to compound the gloominess of the place, it was set well back from the roadway.

Only lovers on Sunday night, lost in happy oblivion in one another's arms, could overlook the fact that they might be propagating the species in pagan territory. For they would know that, owing to ancient enmities, it was the one place, along with the rear of the barrack gate, that was safe from a marauding cleric's blackthorn.

However, I was present in the day room that night as the two night-duty men prepared to depart for Mount Catherine. They knew of the rumours circulating, but put a brave face on it. Cronin, they said, privately, was a phoney, full of bluff and bluster, but hollow inside. They harboured only contempt for him. But then this denial that trouble was imminent made it easier for them to face darkness, tedium and all manner of uncertainty, despite their mutual antipathy and whatever demons lurked within them.

Each had his own routine before he left. Byrne visited the superintendent's lonely wife in her quarters to check if she wanted anything, apart that is from her all too frequently absent husband. I was never present to observe Byrne's bedside manner, his therapeutic style, but then the hardest of men can feign a soft side, especially when given a command to present themselves nightly at the side of the boss's wife who, in her distress, seemed to find even Byrne's presence comforting. Mother told me she was present once when the superintendent returned with two

young women in tow to whom he had given a lift in his car.
Somewhat drunk, he instructed his long-suffering wife to serve
the young ladies tea. As soon as the tea was drunk, she gave
Byrne, who had been sitting up with her, the terse command,
'Now, Jim, will you please drive the ladies home'.

But on that particular day Byrne's normal routine had been
disrupted for, to much hilarity in the barracks, he had been forced
to rise early from his bed to accompany the superintendent to
a place called Killenaule, a few miles east of Cashel in south
Tipperary. This was famous hound-coursing territory and their
mission was to lobby an official for a short slip for one of their
hounds in an upcoming coursing meeting. This would allow
the animal in question an advantage over his rival for, given his
fierce burst of speed over a short distance, he would be able to
crack the screaming hare's neck and tear it limb from limb, to
the delight of the bellowing crowd, long before his rival arrived
on the scene. And thus he would have not only won the contest,
but also conserved energy for later rounds.

Judging by Byrne's hangover that night, their visit must have
been a resounding success. Most likely the pair had stopped at
a few watering holes on the return journey and, given that Dan
was at as low an ebb as I'd ever seen him, one thing was certain:
the two night-duty men would have in common on that night,
a very ugly mood indeed.

Ironically, before Dan was ready to depart, he took what
one might call the opposite path and, as he did most evenings,
visited our household on the other side of the vast four-storey
building, to help the younger children with their homework.
His particular style with the children I had observed from time
to time, and it was a joy to behold. Even when it was obvious

that he was in rather poor form, he was gentle and patient with
them. As a rule, he declined Mother's invitation to sit or take
tea, or even to remove his overcoat, as if it would be impolite
and intrusive. Instead, he bent immediately over the shoulder
of each of the four younger children in turn and clearly enjoyed
their laughter, as they competed for his attention.

But that night his smiling self was absent. He was sombre and,
sensing this, the children were quieter than usual. In happier
times, when asked, he always sang for us, without the slightest
hesitation 'Lili Marlene', 'Bonny Mary', and at Christmas-time,
'Silent Night', 'Ave Maria' and 'White Christmas'. I felt that
these visits compensated him for having to leave his own large
young family, of whom, I had gained the impression, he was
the third eldest. And, at such an unhappy time for him, how he
must have missed them. And how too they no doubt admired
him and hoped one day to emulate him, ever since he had passed
out with flying colours from the police-training depot. It was
probably for their sakes that he felt he had to struggle on, despite
all the troubles besetting him.

Mother adored him, as if he was another son. She often asked
him if he had ever thought of becoming a teacher, so attentive
was he to the younger children. His reply was always the same,
'Ah, Missus, I wouldn't have the qualifications.'

However, as night duty took its toll of him, more and more,
she was full of concern. Many a morning the barrack cook, also a
mother, rushed in, showing her how Dan's socks were dripping wet
after night duty. And they would confer together, looking pained
and sad and all but shedding tears in their distress on his behalf.

On that final particular night, however, Dan came in, as was
his custom, and Mother could see he was more serious than usual.

'Have you heard from your mother lately?' she asked him softly.

'She does not have much time, Missus,' he answered wanly, and then added, 'She has all the others to look after.'

'I'm sure she would love to see you.'

'Ah, Missus,' he answered, as he continued to help the children, 'I'm too tied up at the moment—maybe in the summer.'

I accompanied him as he left our family quarters, on the right-hand side of the barracks proper, and we went together to the barrack day room. Unusually for Dan, he lapsed into silence. He seemed to be in a mental world all his own. As we crossed the lawn, the rain poured down and I could hear his shoes squelching. That did not surprise me because they were the only pair of shoes he had, and earlier I had heard the barrack cook say to Mother that his shoes were 'in flitters'. But he did not seem to notice. He never put much store on material things, not even shoes.

He appeared tense and anxious as we climbed the barrack steps. He was probably wondering, given Byrne's absence all day and the likelihood that he would have consumed a fair amount of alcohol, about what sort of humour his colleague would be in that night. We paused before entering. Concerned about him, I asked him gently, 'Will you be alright?'

He looked me in the eye before answering, and, not for the first time, he seemed to be in a daze, his eyes expressionless, slightly staring. As he answered me, he made an extraordinary, unforgettable gesture. He moved his right hand to caress, ever so lightly, the bulge in his greatcoat pocket. That, I knew, was where he carried his gun. In reply, he said, without changing his vacant expression, 'I can look after myself.' I wondered, rather taken aback, what he could have meant, not so much about what he had said, but by that perplexing gesture. I knew him too well to conclude that it was some ill intent. I believed it to be more a sign of fear, almost a disabling fear of what could happen that night. And, as we entered the day room, my anxiety was intensified.

Byrne was pacing the room, glancing at his watch. One of the proper ways to perform duty was, of course, to be on time, and no one was better at pointing this out than Byrne. No words passed between the men, and the married man who was barrack orderly for that day, noting yet again the awkward silence, looked at me and knowingly threw his eyes up to heaven. Given his penchant for writing verse, Dan may well have had a way with words, but Byrne had a way with silences, and in this particular situation it appears that words could not compete. For Byrne knew, especially in the context of doing duty with a junior, that silence was an intimidation and it gave him control. And control he knew was power.

And so, having asserted his dominance in the partnership, Byrne, looking self-satisfied, was ready to depart. He had prepared for most eventualities except, ironically, for a possible shoot-out, for, yet again to the dismay of the onlooking barrack orderly, he shoved his Webley upside down into the right-side hip pocket of his greatcoat. To compound the felony, as it were, he took hold of his walking stick in his right hand and flashlight in his left, which meant he had no hand free in the case of an emergency. Dan was not encumbered by sartorial or other accessories and, unlike Byrne, who wore his own wellingtons, Dan would squelch his way into the night once more.

By clearing his throat, Byrne indicated to his young partner that he was departing and that he had better follow. This Dan duly did for, like a blind man being led by his dog, he had no other option. I heard their footfalls as they tramped down the barrack steps and I heard too the rain still pouring relentlessly down. In my mind's eye I followed them on their way. Their footfalls got fainter and fainter as they left the barracks and headed towards the crossroads. I knew, having seen their routine so often before, that on feeling buffeted by the winds, they would tighten the straps of their caps firmly under their chins and tug the collars of their greatcoats high about their ears, for it wasn't a night for a dog to be outside.

With the continuing downpour, I knew, moreover, that they would soon feel the damp penetrating their greatcoats for they had not been issued with waterproof capes, nor proper boots or wellingtons. Yet it was vitally important, indeed obsessively insisted upon by the authorities, that each morning all officers paraded clean-shaven, buttons shining and trousers creased.

Given the unrelenting deluge and the high wind remaining unabated, it occurred to me that they could be castaways from a shipwreck in a violent sea, struggling to survive the many elements that sought to overwhelm them.

But, whatever the weather conditions, one thing I knew for sure. As soon as they were out of earshot of possible eavesdroppers, Byrne would warm to his favourite theme, which was the proper way to perform duty. And Dan, yet again, would bite his lip and hold on resolutely to that ill-fitting cap of his and hope that Byrne's tirade, together with the storm, would soon blow over.

At most, on such a night, they would meet a postman or two, also uniformed officers of the State and bound by duty to defy the weather and head for the mail train due in Pallas station an hour or so before midnight. They would ensure that exchanges with such men, however, were perfunctory, with just a brief reference to the poor weather. For they would wish to be careful to give the impression that, far from being at loggerheads with one another, all was well with the world.

After a time, having by now got quite a load off his chest, Byrne would be feeling better. But Dan would not, for without great risk he could not dare answer Byrne back, being as he was a mere recruit and, unlike Byrne, having no friends in high places. And how that must have deepened his frustration for, the truth was that Dan was now, as never before, a man trapped.

Moreover, given the rumour then circulating of an imminent bloody resolution to the land row, the sight he would have seen that night must have intensified his fears; indeed, it may have even troubled Byrne, if ever he noticed such things. For, standing in a field on their right in all its starkness and silhouetted against a dark, wet and windy sky, was the ruin of Kilduff castle. It had a gaping hole where its guts should be and was inhabited as always by a variety of shrieking birds. The sight of it, together with the shrill sounds emanating from it, made it not a little frightening, especially at night. It stands there still like a massive animal on its last legs, with the screaming birds circling like vultures, as if waiting gleefully for the final collapse of their magnificent, yet mortally wounded, prey.

But it was that ugly hole in its midriff, no doubt blown away by a barrage of cannonballs in some conflict centuries before, which would have reminded those two men of how vulnerable they were that night. For they wore no breastplates, no bulletproof vests, no armour or other bodily protection, making them, if the worst came to the worst, sitting ducks.

With these worries put aside, at least for a time, they would march up the long gravelled driveway leading to the Kennedy mansion, and the crunching sound of their footfalls on the deep gravel, once more, would inform the Kennedys, as they prepared for bed, that their protectors had indeed arrived. And though they had never bothered to get to know the men, no doubt they slept all the sounder when aware they were on guard.

I was conscious, however, that when they entered through that high steel gate, in view of all that had happened and all that was rumoured, the tension within them could well be extreme that night. They would be in the midst of dripping trees, bushes and stinging briars, and surrounded by an extremely high boundary wall. And, if there were not enough ill omens already, as I looked north, darker clouds than I had ever seen before hung over the area 'like baleful clouds of doom'. It was as if the gods had willed them to be there, to preside over whatever happened that night.

I knew that once they were inside that gloomy orchard the reality of those two men's lives would strike home and the reality too of their relationship, for how they had already spent nine months there, without strangling one another, I never could fathom. I once asked Dan, tentatively, what in God's name, if anything, they talked about all night and I came up against a brick wall. It was hardly likely that they temporarily buried the hatchet and talked of home, or gazed skywards and asked with Joxer Daly, 'What is the stars?'

It was, in fact, very much later that the secret emerged of how they put down the time, despite their animosity towards one another, and it left many stunned, not least the Kennedys. But that night their unusual coping strategy, alas, never had a chance of being put in train before the men were engulfed and the land row resolved in an instant of madness.

CHAPTER 20

Did I hear shots or was it a dream? Back in the family quarters, I sat up in bed in some alarm and listened intently. It could have been only a short time after midnight. There was no sound save for the wood pigeons cooing contentedly in the old churchyard opposite. I upbraided myself for being so foolish and on edge, and tried to get back to sleep. But no sleep would come. I twisted and turned and eventually found myself drifting.

No sooner did I resume a deep sleep than a loud knocking on the barracks door awakened me again. This time I knew it was not a dream. It was not all that unusual at weekends when acutely distressed folk, following assaults, fist fights, family feuds or drunken brawls, came looking for help to the barracks, but it was not quite the weekend and I had never before heard knocking so insistent. I was convinced it had to do with the shots I thought I had heard earlier.

I jumped out of bed and went silently to the landing window that overlooked the barrack entrance. I opened the window slightly, the better to see and hear what was amiss. I could see the vague outlines of three human forms and was sure, from the glimpse I caught of a peaked cap, that one was a police officer. I knew that the barrack orderly was severely afflicted with arthritis and hated these late intrusions, for on the stroke of midnight, with difficulty, he usually dragged down his old steel bed from upstairs and assembled it beside the phone, and then, with all the ferocity that his aching frame could muster, slammed home the bolt on the front door. I heard him then shouting out, in his unmistakable West of Ireland tones, 'Who's there?' Only the previous week he had told me that, one night not long before, while reading *Dracula* late by a dim light, a bat had flown in the window and so frightened him, as if it were a vampire, that, despite his affliction, he leapt out of bed, as the bat clattered about the room, sometimes, he said, hitting him in his head and face.

In answer to his call, I heard a muffled voice from outside which he seemed to recognize, and then the steel bolts being violently withdrawn. I watched as the group entered immediately and the huge door was banged shut again. I waited for a time, hoping that some sound from within might give me a clue as to the reason for this late night visitation, but I heard nothing. And so, shivering with cold or fear or perhaps both, I returned to bed, my mind in turmoil. I knew in my heart that there might have been a simple explanation, perhaps nothing more momentous than an officer returning with someone wishing to make a phone call in a case of a family illness or accident.

But sleep was slow to come now. And when finally it did, I was assailed by nightmares that I always experienced when I went to bed seriously worried about something, and these ran to a pattern. They usually involved my seeing the room in a state of disarray, the chaos mirroring my inner turmoil. Eventually, from sheer exhaustion, I dropped off to a deeper sleep, but so alert were my senses that it took only the first chink of daylight through my window to awaken me again, probably around 6 a.m.

I went once more to the landing window and received a

shock. There were cars everywhere outside the barrack entrance. Alarmed anew, I concluded that the shots I had heard in the night must after all have been real, for the little group of men outside the gate were brandishing notepads and pens and that told its own story. They were newsmen and I knew in my heart they would not be there if there had not been a fatality.

I dressed quickly and, before slipping out the back door, checked Father's room. He was not in his bed and that was ominous. My path was blocked by a heavily built, plain-clothes man wearing a trench coat, as I tried to enter at the rear door of the barracks. The bulge under his left shoulder spoke for itself. Unsmiling, he told me curtly, 'There's been a shooting. There's no further information.' I reflected as I departed that 'tecs', as Father called them, were indeed a tough breed, a different animal from the average garda.

It was the same story at the front entrance. The newsmen were still outside stamping their feet and walking up and down, trying to keep warm. A second inscrutable tec commanded the entrance and he too was unforthcoming: 'There's been a shooting; there's nothing more to say.' Anxious and worried, I returned to our family quarters.

Mother was preparing breakfast and I could see from her sad, quiet demeanour that she had heard bad news. That was clear from her eyes and her pallor and I judged she had been up in the night. I told her what I'd heard.

'Your father will be in later,' she replied, not looking me in the eye.

'What happened?'

'We don't know yet,' she said, the royal 'we' suggesting that she and Father must have conferred during the night.

I went to Cunningham's shop for news and discovered more than I had bargained for. The national newspaper was just in and the front-page headline shocked me. 'Garda Shot at Farm', it simply said. The location was given and a history of the land row that, it noted, had been simmering for years. The time was given as soon after midnight, around the time I thought I had heard shots. I fought back some tears, as I returned home avoiding several little groups looking shocked and sad.

I was no sooner back home than Father rushed in looking flushed and weary. 'We want you both', he said to Mother and me, 'to come in for prayers', and seemed unable to utter the name of the man for whom we would pray, but by now that man's identity was fast becoming common knowledge. All morning rumours had been rife about the area, some naming Dick Kennedy as the victim, others Cronin, in a shoot-out with the guards. Now we knew, but so numbed were we that many of us were disbelieving.

I watched the cortège, a humble old truck bearing the remains of the dead man, drive into the barrack yard. It was a gateway through which many a victim's remains had been brought over the years, going back to the land wars and probably beyond. Some of those had died ill-prepared, and in such a gruesome manner that many in the village believed that their ghosts, unable to find peace, still appeared there late at night, especially on the wilder winter nights.

We assembled outside at the rear entrance to the building proper. The truck bearing the dead man's remains was followed by two small cars, one containing the superintendent and his wife, the second, relatives of the dead man. The Kennedys were nowhere to be seen. The men removed the body, which was covered by a white sheet, and motioned to us to follow. The body was now laid slowly on two tables drawn together in the washing-up room, beside which, a few paces away, was the barrack kitchen. As the body was laid down, I saw clearly the dead man's naked back, with two deep gashes on the left upper side. My tears became uncontrollable. I had never seen in the cinema or theatre a depiction of Christ's body been taken down from the cross, but the image I saw at that moment was uncannily close to what I had always imagined it might be like. And, as the body was laid down fully, I saw the dead man's face. It was James Byrne.

The barrack cook, with her rosary beads, led the prayers and, as I glanced around at the sea of faces, all looked profoundly shocked. Byrne, I heard many say, was a harmless man. Dan always preferred to describe him as 'a hard man'. As the prayers concluded, one man alone did not seem to share our sadness. He was a bread van driver, a boorish individual, from what in the barracks they called the 'wild west'. Approaching the dead man's brother, instead of offering sympathy, he blurted out his venom, almost spitting on the corpse in the process, 'That will take all the badness out of him,' he said. Those who heard were shocked and Father quickly ushered out the driver. It seems he had once quarrelled with Byrne over some trivial issue. Arrogant through ill-gotten wealth, the bread van driver was known to bear grudges, and even the children in the village gave him a wide berth. He had disgraced himself yet again.

It was several hours before Byrne's body was placed in a coffin and lifted into a motor hearse that had come from the city. And then, as it moved slowly out of the barrack yard, heading for Byrne's home place in the south-east, many of us in the yard crossed ourselves as a last mark of respect. In death a man's flaws are usually put aside, at least for a time. All those standing around grieving then regrouped into little huddles and the speculation began as to what exactly had happened the night before. We did not have to speculate for long. No sooner had Byrne's body departed the village than the news blackout was lifted. Two pieces of information reached us simultaneously, one from the railway station, stating that Timmy Cronin, together with bag and baggage, had left on a late morning train. Many eyebrows were raised in surprise, even disbelief. But then the real bombshell hit us, for we heard that which many of us had secretly feared: a young garda had been charged with murder. And, after that news, all of us in the village who knew Dan and loved him would never be the same again.

CHAPTER 21

D an's misfortune was that he had had too many burdens to bear, especially for one so young. First and foremost, he was an outsider and when he came first had much of the casual cruelty, often reserved for the outsider, visited on him. But then, most crucially, he failed to confront his obsessions; instead, he allowed them to rule him and that can be fatal. And to compound his difficulty, he was possessed of that unique sensibility that all poets are burdened with and along with that, as a rule, goes a temperament that is no mean foe when life turns sour. But, worst of all, he had the rigour of fate to contend with and may actually have believed, through some uncanny gift of insight which I never quite understood, that he would die young, very probably at the hands of the State and in the most humiliating manner that our vengeful species has yet devised.

Already, in the barracks and in the police establishment generally, ranks were closing, wagons circling, use whatever metaphor you like, for there was no way blame for the tragedy would be allowed to attach to anyone but the perpetrator. If such were allowed to happen, the careers of many long-serving officers, who were Dan's colleagues, would be blighted. And, no matter what excuse he offered, I had the impression that they would insist that his desperate act had been carried out in cold blood and that the question of provocation, or other mitigating factors, simply would not arise. And that phrase 'in cold blood', I knew, would be bandied about all week, to ensure that any doubters were made to acquiesce.

In other words, they wanted what they called an open and shut case, one that would enable them to secure a quick charge and conviction, keep the top brass happy and perhaps win a few promotions for some of the more junior members of the serious crime branch of the Garda Síochána. And so, emboldened by the influence of the hard men from that particular squad, they now viewed the youngster as no more than a greenhorn who had shamed himself and the force, and who was never tough enough for the job anyway, and therefore was expendable.

Given this as the direction the investigation took, it was no wonder that Dan Duff twenty-four hours later found himself on a capital charge. And, since he had not yet had the benefit of legal representation, and was physically and mentally devastated, he must have been easy meat for his interrogators. Indeed, I heard later that they even attempted to write his testament for him, as one would help a schoolboy with his homework, all the while assuring him that they had only his best interests at heart. I winced in agony when I heard that some of these men, his one-time colleagues, had stripped him of his uniform, ceased to address him by his first name and brusquely escorted him to the cells below, just beside the dining hall, where more than once I had heard him sing his heart out for them.

But it was Father's riposte to my attempt to speak up for my friend that hurt me most of all: 'Do you not think, Dad, that he is being hard done by?' I asked him, in my dismay and frustration.

'Ah, what would you know about it, boy?' he shot back

dismissively. 'As soon as I put him in the cell, he hopped into his bunk, without saying a single prayer.'

Father, while no great admirer of some clergymen, was loyal to his Maker.

Mother, however, came down firmly on my side, repeating the main sentiment being expressed around the village: 'Sure, he was blackguarded from the very first day he came here,' she said tearfully.

To this, Father was silent and he never afterwards discussed the matter with me. He may have had a reputation for being a good storyteller, but he seemed to keep his own counsel to an extraordinary degree on all worrying official matters.

However, as the investigation came towards an end, I gained the impression that all the local officers' statements were being scrutinized to ensure that they excluded any reference to the prevailing culture in the barracks that had led to the tragedy. No reference would be made to the occasional heavy drinking by some of the members at the station, to Byrne's considerable involvement with the super's greyhounds, which were kennelled in the out offices of the barracks, against regulations, or to foot-dragging by headquarters staff, who long before had promised to replace the two men on night duty, whom everybody knew were well nigh exhausted.

Meantime, Dan had been hung out to dry, forced to serve nine months, seven nights a week without a break on night duty, as if they were testing his survival capacity against all the odds. There was a rule that no officer should spend more than six months on continuous night duty, but one of Dan Duff's problems was that he was too willing and, as a result, was exploited. It was small wonder, then, that the locals who met him in the street towards the end saw a pale, gaunt youth with a gut-wrenching cough and the look of a man, they said, who may have caught that deadly affliction known as 'the bug', the appellation of the time for tuberculosis. To their credit, however, the Kennedys—whose recounting of the night's events and formal statements were by now common knowledge—refused point blank to have their testimony altered in any way. They were preparing for bed, apparently, when they heard shots. Soon an anguished voice shouted up to their bedroom window, 'Are you in bed, Mr Kennedy? ... Get up quick ... I shot James Byrne after we had a terrible row ... I think he's dead.' When they opened the front door, their statement went on, Dan rushed into the hall very agitated, a gun still in hand. He asked for something to drink. Mrs Kennedy who, evidence given later indicated that she had spoken to him on a previous occasion, asked him if he had meant to murder his colleague and he replied, 'Oh good God no!' And then he asked, 'What will happen to me now? Will I be hanged?' And I could not but believe that all his adult life, perhaps because of something that had happened to him in childhood, that dread of death on the gallows may have been his abiding fear.

In effect, Ellen Kennedys' statement, far from indicating that Dan's action had been carried out in cold blood, suggested that it was more likely to have been done in a fit of uncontrollable anger, probably after severe provocation. It appears, however, that this was at odds with police establishment thinking, and inevitably Ellen Kennedy came under some pressure to water down her sympathy for Dan, implied in her statement. But she would not budge. Notwithstanding this, the investigation team pressed ahead with a capital charge, deeming themselves to be the experts, and disregarding whatever anyone else said. It seemed to have been instinctive for these men, desensitized by the daily grind of dealing with such situations, to brush aside, if it suited them, objective facts and seek their pound of flesh.

And so, the case of the Kennedys apart, diluting of any evidence favourable to Duff proceeded apace in the barracks. Hollis, for example, who slept in the dormitory with the two men, was known earlier to have said openly that Dan quite often came under relentless nagging from Byrne, but what would Hollis testify in court? As we shall see, in his evidence he was to say that 'They were always on friendly terms'. Hollis had been got at.

But when the news of the shooting broke in the barracks, what was disappointing was the reaction of McCabe, over whom a cloud hung because of his preference for the company of young boys. The barrack orderly apart, he was the first man out of his bed when the news came in not much more than an hour after the shooting. He found Dan, head in hands, distraught as the full import of what he had done began to dawn on him. He told McCabe his story, hoping perhaps for some flicker of understanding and sympathy. He told him that, following a savage row, Byrne appeared to go for his gun, as he had done before in the course of an argument, and that he, Dan, as he put it, lost his head, and fired in self-defence. But when he told McCabe that he had fired twice, McCabe dispensed instant justice. Rounding on the youngster, he said, 'I would believe that only for the second shot.' In other words, he took it upon himself to act as judge and jury, in effect telling Dan to his face, soon after the incident, that he was guilty. Judas had spoken. It was writer Graham Greene, and I paraphrase him, who once wrote that 'a poet is a victim, a man given over to an obsession'. I came to believe that if, indeed, Dan was obsessive, it had to do with his fear of treachery and, judging by how some of his colleagues in the barracks were now dealing with him, how justified he was.

There was no doubt where the bulk of the villagers' sympathies lay. They were always unhappy about much that went on in the barracks, but were never very vocal about it. Commenting on the tragedy, one of their number expressed their collective sentiment best. Referring to Dan, he said, echoing Mother's verdict, that he was blackguarded from the first day he had come. And there was little doubt that if the jury in the upcoming trial was drawn from the local area, instead of Dublin, the 'in cold blood' theory would be dismissed out of hand. In the event, not a single witness was called by defence counsel for Duff, not even Miss Coffey from Coffey's public house, in whom he confided most of all. Nor was Dr McEnery deemed important enough to ask to give evidence on his behalf, the man Dan had consulted once about his bad cough and to whom he might have disclosed other vital information about how night duty with Byrne was affecting, not only his physical body, but his state of mind as well. Meantime, incredibly, some twenty-one witnesses were called for the prosecution.

And so, it seemed to me at that point that the implications for my friend of the charge that he now faced might indeed mean that he would indeed die young. A survey once carried out showed that only stuntmen and gliding instructors died younger than poets, while deep-sea divers lived longer. But I was always certain of one thing about poets and that was that cold blood does not run in their veins. On the contrary, they are known to be men and women with an excess of feeling and passion in their make-up. They are not violent people: instead, they turn their anger inwards and as a result very many die by their own hand.

Indeed, so uniquely fragile is their sensibility that it was documented a long time ago. For somewhere in the Bible, I recall noting, they were described as a 'touchy breed'. And, if pushed to the limits of their endurance, as the great poet Pushkin was, they can become obsessed with a desperate need to break free from whatever tyranny besets them. But, crucially, and it is an important distinction, they seek release, not reward or revenge, and in so doing are more likely than the average man or woman to lose control and strike out blindly without considering the consequences. And if, in the process, they take the life of the man or woman who is tormenting them, terrible as that might be, it should nevertheless, I believe, be deemed a lesser crime than an act carried out with cold premeditation, for reasons of hate, revenge, lust, gain or jealousy.

But, all that notwithstanding, one conclusion now seemed inescapable. Given all that was stacked against him, my friend Dan looked to be a doomed man. Fate in the end, it seemed, would not be denied.

CHAPTER 22

'We had', he said, 'been fighting for some time. It's a dirty story. It will all come out now.' Ironic words spoken by my friend to the Kennedys on the lonely walk from the farm to the barracks on the night of the tragedy after the full import of what he had done began to sink in, and some vague sense of self-possession was returning to him.

I reflected long on those sentiments of his which, it seemed to me, were the almost philosophical words of a man who had already shown and expressed some remorse, and a man, moreover, from whom a great burden had been lifted, and for whom thoughts of consequences were very much secondary. It was not, I felt, revenge, retribution or reward of any sort that he had sought by his desperate act, but release from the tyranny that had been threatening his very sanity and under which he had laboured for so long.

And those words of his suggested that he believed that when the full story came out, it would gain him some measure of understanding of how he had come to be driven to such a violent act, some understanding of how his situation had become unendurable. Indeed, most probably he had, before the tragedy, explored in his mind every possible means of extricating himself with honour and without further humiliation from his dire predicament. But there were, alas, no formal grievance procedures to which he could resort, and so, sad and tragic though it was, some such outcome had become inevitable.

But the ironic part was that in his belief that 'It will all come out now', he was naive, for come out it most certainly would not, no matter how dirty or otherwise the full story may have been and for the good reason that it would have seriously embarrassed too many people in high places, would have threatened their vital interests and may have caused heads to roll. No, sadly for him, it would not 'all come out now'. It would be consigned to the place where all unsavoury and disconcerting details are often consigned: it would be swept under the carpet. Dan might well have believed, as many of his unique disposition and sensibility do, that the truth will always out. Well, it might one day. But not yet.

And so it was with heavy heart that I made my way down the Dublin quays on a late autumn morning. As I neared that vast cluster of buildings known as the Four Courts, I gazed up at the scales of justice suspended high over them, which symbolize the fine balance those courts must strive to achieve. But knowing, as I did, the sham the proceedings about to begin in the Central Criminal Court were likely to be that week in September 1946, in my anger and frustration I wished I could have grabbed a brick and tossed it on to one side of those same scales, so as to reflect what was really likely to happen. For I knew that, far from balance being achieved, it would be a travesty. And, with a second life at stake as a result of the ineptitude, moral cowardice and self-serving trickery that brought about the end of the first, I found the prospect profoundly depressing.

I was no sooner seated than the prosecuting counsel entered, looking grave and self-important. He was bewigged, as were all his legal colleagues, and they strutted about with armfuls of files that I knew contained for the most part half-truths, if not downright lies. All the pomposity and posturing soon began to irritate me, especially when I knew how ill-informed these people were about the reality of what had gone on for those past two years in that north Munster village.

But then I knew many of these gentlemen believed in their hearts that for the most part they were groping blindly after a truth they did not discover half the time because there were so many, even among their own ranks, trying to thwart them, and quite often succeeding. This was why they had to dress up the proceedings with as much ceremony and formality as possible, to try to lend the thing some semblance of credibility.

Prosecuting counsel soon rose to present the case for the State. It was quickly obvious that he was not going to get into the fine detail of the background, where the real meat that had brought about the tragedy was hidden. For, with policemen investigating fellow policemen from their very own ranks, if he dared delve deep, he knew he might reveal material that would be likely to damage rather than advance his own case.

He told us first of the land row and then of the police protection, the hours on duty and the fact that both men were carrying revolvers and twenty-four rounds of ammunition. He went on to state how the Kennedys had heard the men cross the yard as usual, and soon after they heard shots, and shortly after that the young garda came to the house and, shouting up to their window, gave them the horrific news. He stated that the Kennedys admitted that the officer who rushed into their hallway had a gun still in hand. However, the prosecuting counsel omitted to remark upon the excited state in which the

Kennedys had found the young garda, as he pleaded with them, 'For God's sake, will you give me a drop of whiskey or a drop of brandy?' Nor did counsel make any reference to Ellen Kennedy's question to Dan at that time, 'You didn't intend to murder your colleague, did you?' To which he replied, 'Oh good God no!' If counsel had mentioned these important facts, in the eyes of the jury they might have undermined the 'in cold blood' theory and even saved Dan from the threat to him that he had feared most all his life. But that would not have been in the learned counsel's interest. He wanted an eye for an eye.

Continuing, the counsel told how the superintendent, accompanied by a priest, had gone to the scene, where they found Byrne's body with his gun still in his hip pocket, fully loaded. He went on to state that although the accused had given three separate accounts to different officers about what had happened, they all tallied. He told us further that the accused had 'a certain amount of stout drunk', but said nothing about how much the deceased man had drunk and where and with whom he had drunk it. That might have helped to reveal something of the superintendent's competence and character and, in so doing, undermined the learned gentleman's own case.

Immediately after, counsel uttered the most extraordinary piece of misinformation when he said, 'The men were on friendly terms most of the time.' The truth was that, since Dan had borrowed Byrne's bicycle without permission, Byrne had not spoken to him for four days and they were thereafter very uneasy colleagues indeed. That unease became profound when they had to endure one another for most of the nine months on arduous armed night duty. And so, I fear, the learned counsel, not for the first time that day, was being economical with the truth.

He then summed up the prosecution case. The prosecution, he said, 'is not aware of any motive sufficient for the killing, or any motive which might excuse it in any way. It is necessary for the prosecution to find a motive but the prosecution is saying that the shooting was not accidental, that it was deliberate and that there is nothing to justify it or even excuse it. There is only one person who can say exactly what happened and that is the accused man because he was the only person there when the shooting took place. There is only one inference to be drawn . . . that the accused shot Garda Byrne intentionally, and that the shooting was deliberate.'

Finally the counsel drew attention to a number of facts that, he maintained, bolstered the prosecution case: 'It was a dark night and the accused must have been very close to Garda Byrne in order to place his shot so accurately; it was quite unnecessary for the accused man to be so near Garda Byrne except he wanted to kill him in the way he did. It was too much of a coincidence; the shots were through his heart. The accused man has said that Garda Byrne went to his right-hand pocket and that he, the accused, thought that he was going to pull a gun, and that he pulled his own gun and shot him. The gun was not in his right-hand pocket and the accused must have known this. If Garda Byrne did attempt to go for his gun, the accused was not entitled as a matter of law to shoot him in the way he did.'

The case for the State now concluded, the first person into the witness box was Ellen Kennedy. She told of having heard shots on the night and of admitting Dan to the house soon after and her conversation with him. Her tone suggested that she harboured not a little sympathy for the young man and her husband Dick's subsequent evidence concurred with hers. No one was in a better position, in the immediate aftermath of the tragedy, to gauge the

sincerity or otherwise of Dan's explanation. Indeed, the manner
in which she phrased her question to him at that direful moment,
'You didn't intend to murder your colleague, did you?' suggested
that she would be surprised, given his demeanour, if he had so
intended. As I watched her, in her customary elegance of dress,
stepping down from the stand, it occurred to me that it was
unlikely there would be many others that week with sympathy
in their hearts for the accused.

Three officers from the station were then called to give evidence
for the prosecution. The barrack orderly on the night was one of
the married officers who lived outside the station, and he said
that he had admitted Dan, together with the Kennedys. He
spoke of his exchanges with him, stating that Dan had buried
his face in his hands beside the window when he came in. The
barrack orderly emphasized that he did not see a flashlight in
Dan's possession, although, in Dan's statement to him, he stated
that he had used a flashlight to search for a pear from a pear tree
before the shooting. Defence counsel was obliged to recall Ellen
Kennedy to rebut the falsehood. She was emphatic. 'Yes,' she
said, 'he had indeed a flashlight when I met him.' The barrack
orderly's efforts to undermine his colleague's evidence, whatever
his motivation, had failed.

McCabe's performance in the witness box was no more edifying.
He restated what he had said in his earlier written testimony: when
Dan told him that he had fired twice, he formed the opinion that
he was therefore guilty of murder and, although it was no more
than an hour after the shooting, he told him so. In reply to the
prosecuting counsel, he stated further that he saw no evidence of
excitement or distress about Dan Duff. It was extraordinary that
McCabe had not waited for due process before condemning Dan.

How, I felt, he may wish one day that his colleagues do not rush to judgment of him, if ever he found himself on trial.

Hollis's evidence, too, was a disgrace and a betrayal. He slept in the dormitory throughout with the two men, and in an earlier statement had spoken of the relentless nagging Dan had suffered at Byrne's hands. But, when in the witness box, all that changed. 'They were always on friendly terms,' he said, only to immediately contradict himself by adding, 'They had a heated discussion one night, but were perfectly friendly the next day.' And so, what from Hollis's lips had formerly been 'a fierce row' had now become 'a heated discussion'. It was truly amazing how these three grown men, in mindless obedience to authority and fearful for their jobs, could morally compromise themselves with such a blatant misrepresentation of important evidence, and in so doing risk sending their colleague to the gallows.

Father was next to be called to the witness box and he spoke at some length about Dan's worsening state of health before the shooting. He did not say, however, whether or not, in his opinion, he suffered physical ill health only or psychological stress as well. Alas, there was no expert testimony given as to Dan's psychological state. 'I suggested to him', Father went on, 'that he go on sick leave, but he did not. I told him the superintendent had also noted his ill health and had recommended him for day duty. He asked what would happen following that recommendation and I told him he would probably be transferred.' Replying to defence counsel, my father continued: 'The accused looked very run down because of the long unbroken spell on night duty, which had been a trial.' However, counsel from neither side questioned why a young police officer should be left so long on night duty, seven nights a week without a break including weekends, for nine months.

There seemed to be a reluctance to question anything that might reflect badly on the police authorities. And so, yet another nail was driven into my friend's coffin.

The superintendent's evidence was taken next. He told the court that he had been called from his home on the night and, when he met the accused in the barrack day room, the officer had said, 'I'm sorry, sir; I could not help it.' The superintendent stated that he went immediately to the orchard at the back of Mount Catherine House and saw Byrne's body and, on returning, charged Dan with murder. When he did so, he said Dan replied, 'Not with malice aforethought.' In the course of his further testimony, the superintendent insisted that he did not regard the night duty as 'onerous'.

There was a pause while we waited for Dan to be called to the witness box. Meanwhile, I reflected on Father's evidence in particular. I felt that he had touched on a key precipitating event that had led to the shooting—his proposed transfer to another Garda station. To be transferred without just cause was always a humiliation. For Dan it was, I came to believe, the last straw. He was being banished, as he would have perceived it, through the collusion of Byrne and the superintendent. He probably saw it as the final treachery. The bully had won and he was to be the victim. His right to his dignity had been taken from him and he had been gradually broken down, for bullies are known not to relent until their victim's spirit is finally crushed. Dan, being something of an artist and therefore a perfectionist, would have, I believe, felt that hurt deeply. I met him face to face shortly after the transfer was mooted and he seemed near to distraction. Noting his state, I asked him, as he went out on duty on that last night, if he would be all right. His answer and the accompanying gesture I shall always remember: 'I can look after myself,' he said. He looked like a man who had been suppressing his anger for a long time. Now, it seemed to me, it was about to reach boiling point.

And so, erect of bearing but gaunt and pale of face, with dark suit and tie, and a *fáinne* in his lapel, my friend and one-time mentor took the stand. 'I could not get any rest,' he said, in response to defence counsel. 'When Byrne and I would go to bed, it would be around six thirty in the morning before we would get to sleep. The noise in the barracks would wake me up and I would remain awake. During the nine months I did not get any break, being on duty every night during the week.'

'Did you find this affected your health in any way?' defence counsel asked.

'I did. I was always tired and depressed and irritable.'

'Did you get wettings?'

'I got many wettings, especially in winter.'

'Byrne's attitude', Dan went on, 'was that he wanted me to be at the farm when he wasn't, but he wanted me to stay with him when he was there, even though in winter the hours were staggered so that we started and finished an hour separate to one another. Sometimes he would go away and leave me and sometimes I would go away and leave him. At other times we would both go off together.'

It was a breathtaking revelation that should have invited detailed exploration by counsel but did not, for it might have revealed the true state of the men's relationship. It had many serious implications, not least because it meant that some of the time the Kennedys did not have any protection at night more visible than their guardian angels. But surprisingly, defence counsel passed quickly on, not daring to dwell on the matter.

The revelation should also have invited the question as to where the men went, for they could not have returned to the barracks when they were supposed to be on night duty. In fact, the men had only one other option which was to go to separate pubs in the area and, being uniformed police officers, they would be admitted after hours to the owners' private quarters and, very likely, offered drinks and given help to dry out their clothes and rest on a couch until daylight.

I presumed ever after that this was what Dan meant by the 'dirty story' which he said, bless his naivety, 'will all come out now', but did not, because no one else would dare reveal such a thing, in court or out of it. And his candour, which he had hoped might have helped him, left me with the extraordinary thought that the man who, very possibly, was facing execution may well have been the most truthful of the entire lot. But then poets are said to have a passion for the truth.

And so Dan Duff continued his evidence. 'Byrne and I had arguments constantly, and sometimes they would blow over the next day. But last month we had a dispute in the kitchen garden of the Kennedy farm about duty. When we were arriving, I told Byrne that if he called me names again, I would hit him. He took out his gun and told me if I attempted to strike him, he would blow my brains out.'

Defence counsel then asked him, 'From your acquaintance with Byrne, did you come to any conclusion about his temper?'

'He was hot-tempered and rather reckless with a gun in hand. He was a tough man.'

'Had you any feeling of hatred or ill will towards Byrne?' counsel enquired.

'None,' Dan replied.

Dealing with the night of the shooting, the accused continued, 'We were on reasonably good terms going out, but as we neared the farm he charged me with being a long time in getting used to duty. I told him I could say the same about him, and added that I thought he did not care because he had the superintendent on his side. He replied by saying that I seemed to expect the same treatment as men longer in the job than myself. I countered by telling him that I suspected him of telling the superintendent about the times I dodged. We were both very angry. We were just coming to the house and were cursing and swearing at one another. We quietened down when we neared Kennedy's window.'

'Byrne', Dan Duff went on, 'moved towards the loft and I went towards the yard. He said, "I'm going in here for a sleep and you can fuck off home if you like." I said I was going for a pear, as I was thirsty. He followed behind me saying, "That's right, be contrary!" I asked him, "How is that being contrary?" He started cursing again at me. I went towards the pear tree and he followed me. He was getting on to me and I was cursing and swearing back at him. I flashed my torch at the tree to look for a pear. He was underneath the tree. He kept getting on to me and said, "You fucking young pup. You were only dragged up. I'll give you a slap in the mouth which you have been looking for for a long time." I said that if there was any slapping to be done, he might not come out of it so handy. I also said that if he did not stop calling me names, I would give him the hiding of his life. He said, "I told you before what would happen if you ever hit me. I will blow your brains out." I had my back to the pear tree and he was facing me. He made a quick motion towards his right-hand overcoat pocket. Then I got panicky. I pulled out my gun and fired at him. I'm not sure when the second shot was fired because I lost my head. I moved quickly towards him and my finger tightened on the trigger for the second shot. He toppled backwards and in the excitement I fired a second shot when he was falling.'

'It was a dark night and yet we were able to see each other up to six or seven feet apart or more. I never thought of the gun until I saw Byrne making a move. I stood for a second looking at him before I realized what was happening. I bent over him and he was jerking on the ground. I caught hold of him by the shoulder and I said, "Jim, are you alright? Can you hear me?" He only groaned. I still had the torch in my left hand and it was shining on his face. I saw he was hurt and I said an Act of Contrition loudly in his ear. Just as I finished the Act of Contrition, he died, although I was not sure. I thought he might not be dead. I thought he might only be unconscious. I ran down to Mr Kennedy.'

Cross-examined by prosecuting counsel, Dan said, 'In training I was not taught to use my revolver as a last resort but was trained in the use of it and about the mechanism and told to use it in self-defence.' To a further question as to whether or not he was a good shot, he said, 'I was a fairly good shot but I thought I would not have to use it, that it was going to come to fists.'

Asked if there was anything preventing him from grappling with Byrne and throwing him to the ground to prevent him from using his gun, he said, 'I never thought of that; it entered my head immediately to use my gun.'

Questioned then by the judge as to what his intention was when he fired, he replied, 'I don't know, My Lord. I just got it into my head to stop him from shooting.' Asked further if he had aimed at Byrne's heart, he said, 'The bullets could have hit anywhere. I just fired two shots at him. I fired at his chest alright.'

The judge then put it to him that firing at his chest was going to kill Byrne, to which Dan replied, 'I never thought of that.'

The prosecuting counsel then addressed the jury. 'If one shot had been fired, the case might have been made that it was unfortunate, but when two shots are fired there is only one intention to infer.'

We paused now for the defence counsel to speak to the jury. While we waited, I realized that the question of the second shot did indeed seem to be crucial. Yet an eminent behavioural scientist whom I interviewed years later about this particular point, remarked, 'When you snap, you snap, and whether it is one shot or ten, it does not much matter.' Regrettably, no one with her qualifications or experience had been invited to give evidence to the court. However, the prolific Canadian crime writer Howard Engel would support her, for he once wrote in a similar context, 'Emotion obliterates conscious choice; it is as though the perpetrator does not exist. The assassin "becomes" the gun or the knife, which then kills apparently of its own volition.'

It was defence counsel's turn to make his case for the defence. 'When you come to consider the self-defence aspect, you should take into consideration the possibility of the accused's judgement having been impaired by nine months of duty night after night without sufficient sleep; the tragedy is that two decent, respectable men, by no means of the criminal class, must have been a bundle of nerves from lack of proper sleep. It was a killing done in anger by two men equally armed. It was self-defence as far as the accused knew it.'

We waited anxiously for the judge to sum up. There was a hush of expectancy. As he rose, there was complete silence. Many had their fingers crossed. Dan looked impassive. 'The question you have to consider', the judge said, 'is not whether the accused intended to kill the deceased but whether at the time he fired the shots he intended to fire them. You will also have to consider whether the shots were fired in self-defence. You have to consider if a reasonable man, placed in precisely the same position as the accused, would have taken the step of firing a deadly weapon at close quarters, with the range not more than six or seven feet, at the outside. You also have to consider if there could be any possibility of firing a second shot in self-defence. If you think that firing a revolver at the man's chest bears any relation to the amount of provocation the accused received, you might come to the conclusion that the power of self-control had been taken so much from the accused that it was manslaughter and not murder.'

When the judge's directions to the jury had concluded, I sensed a favourable response around me, with much murmuring and nodding. He had not excluded the possibility of a manslaughter verdict. But the question of the severity of provocation suffered by the accused was critical and it had not been allowed to emerge except in part, and only from the lips of Dan himself. In the absence of such independent testimony, it was difficult to see how the jury could conclude that Dan had lost the power of self-control sufficiently to justify his actions, and therefore there seemed only the slimmest chance that the lesser verdict would be brought in.

Our wait of an hour and a half for the return of the jury seemed endless. Earlier, one of their number had asked to be excused on the grounds of having a conscientious objection to capital punishment. I could not believe that the rest of the jury and most of the public would go along mindlessly with such a horrific barbarity: revenge by the State on the individual. It seemed to me an entirely inappropriate means of punishing a man for his misdeeds in a supposedly civilized era.

As the jury filed in, I was filled with foreboding. The jury foreman turned towards the judge, who asked him to read out the verdict. Never before had I experienced a moment of such tension. The jury foreman paused. He was pale of face and seemed overwhelmed with emotion. Finally, he spoke with trembling voice, 'Guilty, My Lord.'

There were sobs and cries from Dan's large family and friends. His father had been a sergeant at the Curragh Army Camp, County Kildare. There were seven sons, Dan being the third eldest. Two of his brothers had died as young boys, one of a serious illness, the other when hit by a lorry with his mother looking on. This left the poor woman severely traumatized for a long time. Dan was said, by his school principal at the Dominican college in Newbridge, County Kildare, to have been the most brilliant boy in class. His record, when a year or so in the army, had been above reproach, as it was during his training in the Garda depot.

But now his family had been struck a great blow once more and was devastated. Most people around me in the court were dismayed. I felt numbed. I expected it, but could not believe it now that it had happened. To my mind it was a travesty of justice; it was merciless. To make matters worse, leave to appeal was refused. When I later heard the grounds of the appeal, my conviction was all the more profound that the result was tantamount to a miscarriage of justice. These grounds of appeal were as follows:

1) The learned Judge misdirected the jury in law on the issue of manslaughter by:

a) Not telling the jury that words coupled with a threat of immediate violence by a man armed and capable of carrying out that threat may in law be sufficient to reduce murder to manslaughter.

b) In not properly redirecting the jury in Counsel's objection that the threat in the moments the deceased's hand moved towards the position of his gun should be considered in conjunction with the verbal threats when the jury were considering whether or not there was sufficient provocation to reduce murder to manslaughter.

2) In the admission of the learned Judge of evidence tendered by the prosecution after the close of the prosecution's case which evidence the prosecution could have given on the direct examination of the witnesses recalled.

3) The learned trial Judge did not in his charge to the jury adequately put to the jury the case made in evidence on the part of the accused.

4) In misdirecting the jury in law in not charging them that the accused's intention when firing the first shot was a vital thing for them to consider and that the intention of the accused when firing the second shot should be appraised after considering the first.

5) The trial was unsatisfactory in that in the preliminary remarks to the jury, the learned Judge told the jury that if he was wrong in law he could be set right elsewhere so tending to relieve the jury of their responsibility.

To compound our horror, as if we had not enough absurd ceremony already, the Judge put on a black cap before announcing sentence:

'The sentence and judgment of the court are that it is ordered and adjudged that you Daniel Joseph Duff be taken from the bar of the court where you now stand to the prison whence last you came and that on Wednesday the 11th day of December in the year of our Lord one thousand nine hundred and forty six you be taken to the common place of execution in the prison that you be then confined and that you then and there be hanged by the neck until you are dead and that your body be buried within the walls of the prison in which the aforesaid judgment of death shall be executed upon you. And may the lord have mercy on your soul. Have you anything to say?'

My young and dear friend, paler now, but appearing composed, replied in a firm voice, 'I have nothing to say now, My Lord.'

As he was taken down, he looked at his family with a vague expression of resignation. And then, before he left with the wardens, he turned abruptly towards a tall, dark lady in the body of the court whom I had not noticed before, because the court was so full. He managed for her a courageous, lingering smile. Then he was gone. I glanced across at the young lady as she wiped away some tears, to discover that it was indeed Phoebe Connell. My heart went out to them.

As I left the court, I recalled some lines of Alan Seeger's poem, one of the many that Dan recited for me that first summer after he had come to Pallas, as we sat together in the sun on the barrack steps.

It may be he shall take my hand
And lead me into his dark land
And close my eyes and quench my breath...
But I've a rendezvous with Death
At midnight in some flaming town
When Spring trips north again this year,
And I to my pledged word am true,
I shall not fail that rendezvous.

CHAPTER 23

The length of the drop apparently is everything. Too long a drop and the job would be bungled, as would be the case if the drop were too short. Indeed, this matter of the length of the drop was deemed of such momentous importance that over a century before an eminent academic and reverend gentleman from that great bastion of liberal values, Trinity College Dublin, conducted some fairly extensive research, with the intention, for the advancement of science and thus for the benefit of future generations, of getting the drop length exactly right.

It seems that the Reverend Samuel Haughton was immensely gifted, not only in the field of mathematics but in the sciences and humanities as well. And so, no doubt with the moral and financial backing of that great seat of learning, he wrote a brilliant paper on the subject of the drop, which was immediately acclaimed. It can be seen in Trinity to this day, and it incorporated a table, facilitated by this man's considerable mathematical ingenuity. The paper was entitled 'A Handy Guide for the Hangman'.

The foregoing is just a sample of the sort of thing that assailed me when, one evening in early December 1946, I opened a tabloid newspaper, inspired by the fact that very shortly an act of State-sanctioned vengeance would be perpetrated against a friend of mine, in that other, rather less well-esteemed national institution, Mountjoy Prison.

The paper did not say, however, whether the Reverend Haughton was subsequently knighted by His Majesty for his groundbreaking work or whether some accolade from the international scientific community was bestowed upon him for using his vast and wide learning to push out the frontiers of scientific method by devising a swifter and more efficient means of breaking a man's neck.

But the paper did not spare us, for there was more. It had for a start a screaming headline that said, 'Pierrepoint coming to Town', as if some great Hollywood luminary or eminent international statesman was soon to visit our shores. Mr Pierrepoint was in fact the chief hangman for His Majesty's government in Great Britain, due to come for little more than a weekend, to perform what the paper described as 'a one-off'.

The newspaper went on to tell us that the great man had already 'several hundred scalps under his belt', including those of some of the leading lights of the Nuremberg trials of 1946. It told us further that Mr Pierrepoint made no bones about the fact that he enjoyed his work, that it was a family thing, and that he was proud to uphold the family tradition of doing the job well. Continuing in this vein, the newspaper said that Pierrepoint's success was believed to derive from the fact that, given his 'quick eye, steady hand and cool brain', he was 'an artist of sorts' and had a happy knack, not given to everyone, of carrying out the thing exactly right, of getting the drop length, that is, spot on.

With yet half a paragraph to use up, the paper gave us the cheering information that Pierrepoint accorded such attention to detail that, in advance of the event, he liked to dress up as a prison warden and bring his victim tea and toast. In so doing, he would pretend that he came with sorrow and compassion in his heart, thus duping the wretched victim awaiting his fate. Pierrepoint's objective, apparently, was to get a good look at his man close up, his height, his weight and his neck length. What a charming fellow this Mr Pierrepoint must have been.

But his charm did not end there. It appears that he had stated in the course of interviews that he enjoyed hanging Irishmen in particular because they were so religious that they were well prepared and often eager to meet their Maker. Indeed so compliant were they, according to Mr Pierrepoint, that they sometimes lent him a hand in strapping up their legs tightly and placing a black hood over their heads so that they could not see the chalk mark on the floor marking the trapdoor that would finally plunge them into oblivion.

All night this gruesome picture of what was to happen quite soon had tortured me, preventing sleep. But one angry thought was paramount. And that was that my friend had been duped enough already, and sufficiently humiliated too in his short twenty-two years of life, and though I had never heard of the tables being turned on a hangman and his being dumped head first into the pit below, there was always a first time, and if any man could do it, surely it was Dan. For I knew my friend well and I could not see him going quietly like a lamb to the slaughter. It was simply not in his nature.

And so as I lay awake in my lodgings in the city, coincidentally not much more than a mile from the venue where this obscene act would soon occur, there was pain and frustration in my heart because the only thing I could now do to help him was to pray, and that I did while waiting, often tearfully, as the hour of his doom came closer. As I did so, I thought of Father, who wrote letters endlessly on behalf of other victims of injustice, but knew that there was probably little then that he could do. I even thought of Grian, an ancient Irish goddess of love, who, legend had it, resided on the hill named after her, which overlooked my little village. Had she, I wondered, abandoned Dan too? I realized, however, that, in my desperation, I was merely grasping at straws.

One morning, as the time of Dan's execution drew near, there was a gentle knock on my bedroom door at eight o'clock. My landlady had been the saviour of my sanity during the weeks since the trial. I had found her through an advertisement in the press. She was a woman from another jurisdiction and of a different religious persuasion to myself. She was forced, despite her good education and sensitive and exquisite nature, to take paying guests in those economically straitened times of the mid-1940s.

Soon after I came, I told her my story and we talked for a long time. She had deep brown pools for eyes, the saddest I had ever seen. There was hardly any doubt that she had had a great hurt in her past. She was about forty years old, more than twice my eighteen years, a warm motherly person and she knew that I too was anxious and lonely. And how lucky I was that she was with me at that dreadful time.

One weekend afternoon, when the house was very quiet, but for the two of us, I met her on the landing upstairs. Having recently decorated her large front bedroom, looking out on the sea, she invited me to see it. We stood for a long time together, just inside the door. Our conversation was idle and inconsequential, but it did not seem to matter, we were so comfortable with one another. Sometimes we looked again at the décor, sometimes out to sea. Occasionally we glanced simultaneously at the magnificent double bed just beside where we were standing. I believed it was because of its comforting presence that we remained there until darkness fell. Yet, so inhibited were we, that we dared not mention its presence or admire its soft and elegant covering. Though I was young and inexperienced, I knew then that we were two of a kind, burdened by an excess of inhibition, which could well leave us handicapped for life.

Since that day she had brought me breakfast in bed, despite my protests, on the mornings that I lay in, and how glad I was to hear her quiet knock again that morning, earlier than usual. She may have, I thought, heard me up in the night and knew what I was going through that morning.

By name Euphemia, she was a woman who seemed to live in fear of offending people and when she walked into the bedroom, having enquired if I was well, she placed the tray nervously on the table beside my bed, as if she feared she would spill the tea or knock something over. She was dressed in a snow-white dressing gown and slippers. Her fragrance wafted over me, as if she had just bathed. Normally she withdrew immediately, but that morning she lingered, as if she wished to say something, but could not find the words.

She usually spoke in whispers, choosing her words with extreme care. I sometimes thought, given all that sympathy for others, that she may have been at one time a therapist of sorts and was now doing no more than what she was good at, sharing my pain and, in the process, helping me through an unbearably anguishing time.

She closed the door gently and, fidgeting with the cord of her dressing gown, moved a fraction closer. It crossed my mind for an anxious moment that she may have been about to offer me some more intimate form of consolation than I had hitherto enjoyed with her and for which repressed village life had ill-prepared me. She seemed surprised that I was not in a brighter mood. She looked me in the eye now and there was a tone of disbelief in her voice as she spoke.

'Did you not hear the news on the radio?' she said, her voice rising a little.

'I cannot bear to tune in these mornings,' I answered, wondering what could have animated her so.

'Your friend,' she said, 'your friend,' she repeated, incredulous that I had not heard, 'on the intervention of the Minister, Mr Boland, has been reprieved.'

EPILOGUE

Five years later Dan Duff was a free man. I wanted to meet him, just to say 'Sorry we let you down'. I had resolved to avoid altogether discussing our times back in the village, unless he wanted to. I knew him to be a prolific writer of poetry in the native tongue and I had often wondered if his muse had survived his prison sentence. I hoped to ask him about that too. I had heard he had studied languages while in jail and then gone abroad for a time, but was now doing security work in a Dublin hotel.

I assumed it was unlikely that he had ever had the opportunity or the inclination to exercise his magnificent tenor voice when in prison. How sad that must have been for him. I was determined to meet up with him and resolved to keep my eyes alert in the city at weekends.

I wanted to meet Phoebe Connell too. I had been on the lookout for her constantly, since I had heard that she too had come to work in Dublin. I had no idea what I would say to her. I would have to place my faith in the moment, and hope I would utter something appropriate. I had heard that her relationship with Dan had not survived his imprisonment and I wondered if his release had brought about a reconciliation. I wondered too if Phoebe had the faintest idea of the depth of feeling I had retained for her, which I had had to suppress when she and Dan became lovers. They were the two people who had made my teenage years memorable and I was determined to meet them both. In a way, I felt that my life was on hold until I did so.

Meantime, back in the village, there had been changes. In due course, the Kennedys sold their farm and went to live in a small bungalow in a relatively poor area of northside Dublin. However, when Ellen Kennedy passed on, some years after her husband, it was discovered that the deeds of the disputed land were still in her name. She had, apparently, originally paid for those couple of fields, which had caused so much unhappiness with her very own cash and, as it were, taken them to her grave, as if she hoped this would ensure that her suffering would be the last they would cause.

Garda headquarters moved quickly to transfer most of the men, including the superintendent, from Pallas to stations elsewhere. Father, however, escaped the axe. Houdini had indeed survived and went on to serve eleven years in Pallas, before retiring, when he moved reluctantly to Dublin; and in the mid-1960s when the Pallas farmers, whom he held in high regard, joined their colleagues countrywide to march to Government Buildings in the city, in pursuit of a better deal for farmers, Father marched through the city shoulder to shoulder with one of the Pallas farm leaders, David Dillon, a great friend of his.

I was always curious to know if my father had played any part in Dan's reprieve, but could not find any hard evidence and he never discussed the matter with me. When finally he passed to his reward, however, I did find among his papers a letter from Dan's mother, written in early 1947, a few months after his reprieve. It read as follows:

Dear Sergeant,

I hope yourself and the family are quite well. We still remember how good you were to Dan. He is in splendid health and bearing his incarceration very well. We have become resigned to the sadness of his lot. He said he had heard you had left Pallas so I did not know what to do, as I could not find out if you were still there or not.

I would be glad if you would send on any few belongings of his that are still there. I shall be glad to hear from you and regret having to trouble you in view of all you have done for us. I am sure you have your time occupied enough.

Yours sincerely,
Mary Duff

However, a few years had passed after Dan's release before I encountered him. In the interim, I was fortunate to have secured a job in the offices of a large international company with headquarters in Britain and I was soon to discover that the sort of predicament Dan endured was not that uncommon in workplaces generally.

It was some time after that I came upon Dan Duff in strange circumstances. A major figure in the British arm of the company, for which I worked, came to Dublin. His mission was to take out to dinner nightly three or four young trainee managers to try to assess what sort of management potential we possessed and whether or not it might be necessary to send in some replacements from Britain, if the native breed was not quite up to the mark.

We were told that this man did not take alcohol and that the subject he was most interested in was china. We realized that night as we sat down in the dining room of the Royal Hibernian

Hotel in Dublin's Dawson Street, that it was not clear whether the china in question was the variety from which we would eat our dinners, or that somewhat larger entity, written with a capital C. After duly conferring on the matter, we agreed that we knew little about Wedgwood and even less about the Great Wall, but we would have to, as they say, play it by ear. Two of our Irish group spent several hours in the basement bar of the hotel beforehand, preparing for the ordeal to come. They duly arrived, barely on time in the dining room, their gabardines flapping open and each with a pint of porter in his fist which they plonked down with a splash or two on the exquisite, white linen tablecloth of the Royal Hibernian. Then, after the great man introduced himself to them, they continued, unabashed, the good-humoured conversation they had been having downstairs. To his credit, the Englishman scarcely raised an eyebrow. Eventually we regrouped to hear what the great man had to say. As it turned out, that was very little. At some point our host did indeed raise the question of china. He received little response and in embarrassment at the awkward silence, I blurted out the question to him, 'Have you read its history?' only to receive by way of reply from his eminence, without raising his eyes from his plate, 'No.'

So forgettable was the evening that I recall little else of the actual dinner, but when I entered the hotel foyer to depart, I came face to face with the commissionaire. For a split second I caught his eyes meeting mine. He was thin and wiry and his cap was ill-fitting. Dan Duff's cap never quite fitted him, nor did he ever, I thought, belong in a uniform. Yet there he was, a humble, incongruously dressed commissionaire in a hotel. He wore a greying beard and had aged. But those alert, penetrating eyes I could never forget.

He turned away abruptly, as I tried for a second or two to hold his gaze. Did he recognize me? I shall never know. I was now older, wearing spectacles, and I had put on a little weight. As I walked away, I was regretful, wondering if I should not have at least held out my hand and called his name. I was never to see him again.

My encounter with Phoebe Connell also came about rather unexpectedly not too long afterwards. Never a day passed but I thought of her. She was, after all, my childhood sweetheart and I always believed that a man retains a strong emotional attachment, ever after, to the girl who had first awakened in him, at a tender age, intense feelings of desire. I saw her occasionally as I drove to work in the south city when, in the early mornings, she was coming out of church after Mass. From her pallor and strained expression, I gained the impression that she was an unhappy young lady—now close to thirty years of age—who had not found enduring love and may have still been suffering from her father's cruel and clumsy intervention in her love affair with Dan a decade or more before.

Then one Sunday night I had a stroke of luck. It seemed as if the whole city was going to Bray to dance to the music of a famous bandleader, Mick Delahunty, in the Arcadia Ballroom there. Unaccompanied, I followed the crowd from the city on a single-decker shambles of a bus. The ballroom was packed tight, sweaty and dark. I had regularly attended all the southside hops in tennis and rugby clubs, but never, to my chagrin, had I encountered Phoebe Connell. That steamy night, however, I was largely a bystander and I suffered some moments of intense emotional stress when, in the semi-darkness, I saw one or two tall, dark, young women, resembling Phoebe, being crushed in the arms of far more handsome men than me. However, I stayed until the last dance, and I was sure, despite the vastness of the place, that she was not in attendance.

Downcast, I climbed aboard the last bus out of Bray. I sat in the rear seat of the single-decker bus, the better to survey all those who, like me, had failed to find a prospective lover to escort home. Though seemingly full, the bus halted suddenly, one stop outside Bray. My heart leapt when I identified the young lady about to board. It was indeed Phoebe Connell! I noted that she was no longer the slim, young teenage beauty by whom I had been besotted through my later teenage years. But she was still attractive and she was Phoebe Connell, and that was all that mattered. I could hardly believe my luck. We were both travelling alone. She had not found love, I concluded, nor had I. The gods had smiled on me at last. It was a moment I had waited years for. But then, just as quickly as a feeling of great joy gripped me, came devastation. For, on boarding the bus at the rear, she looked straight at me, without the merest flicker of recognition and went to find a seat at the front.

As we drove towards the city, I toyed with the idea of getting off at the same stop as her. But one hurt, I decided, was enough for one night. So, feeling dejected, I stepped off the bus at Pembroke Road near where I lived. It was then I recalled a former flatmate, by name John, whose girlfriend belonged to a different religion and how each night after the cinema in Rathmines, while seeing her home, he proposed to her and each time she declined his proposal. Love, they say, will find a way, but the young woman probably knew well that if she dared marry outside 'the fold', pleading that she suffered from that strange delirium known as romantic love would cut no ice with the Archbishop, or for that matter, with The Legion of Mary.

John's way of coping was to loudly whistle his way home. I shall always remember hearing him coming up Leinster Road to Grosvenor Square late at night; one of his tunes, if I recall correctly, was the theme song from *The Bridge on the River Kwai*. In those days the city was near silent after midnight, which made it possible to hear him coming from afar. We had dubbed him 'The Nightingale of Grosvenor Square'. His tune would end as he put his latchkey in the door, and then entering, his face downcast, he would say simply, 'No go, lads'. We would grimace in sympathy, unable any longer to find appropriate words of consolation, and all then slope off silently to bed.

And so as I walked up Pembroke Road on that night of the dance, my hopes of renewing my acquaintance with Phoebe Connell dashed, I decided to take a leaf out of John's book. As I went, I found myself reflecting that the poet Patrick Kavanagh strolled along that same stretch of road every day, musing to himself, and I concluded therefore only one air was for me appropriate and I whistled with all the gusto that I could summon. It was Kavanagh's lament for unrequited love:

On Raglan Road on an autumn day I met her first and knew
That her dark hair would weave a snare that I might one day rue;
I saw the danger, yet I walked along the enchanted way,
And I said, let grief be a fallen leaf at the dawning of the day.

· · · ·

On a quiet street where old ghosts meet I see her walking now
Away from me so hurriedly my reason must allow
That I had wooed not as I should a creature made of clay—
When the angel woos the clay he'd lose his wings at the dawn of day.